On comeout
2, 3, 12 los
must make p
a seven If point made, next
throw a come out

Casino Gambling

Other books by Jerry L. Patterson

Blackjack's Winning Formula
Sports Betting
The Casino Gambler's Winning Edge
Blackjack: A Winner's Handbook

Casino Gambling

Winning Techniques For Craps, Roulette, Baccarat & Blackjack

By

Jerry L. Patterson & Walter Jaye

A Perigee Book

To Nancy for making it all happen, and to Yvonne for making it all worthwhile.

Jerry and Walter

We would especially like to acknowledge Gil Stead's work on casino games and systems, much of which contributed to the thoroughness of this book. Once again we want to thank Don Schlesinger for his usual meticulous job of technical editing. We are also grateful to Mary Anne Palladino and Rosemarie Burk for the hours spent proofreading and editing the final manuscript.

J.L.P. and W.J.

A Perigee Book
Published by The Berkley Publishing Group
A member of Penguin Putnam Inc.
200 Madison Avenue, New York, NY 10016

The Putnam Berkley World Wide Web site address is http://www.berkley.com

Library of Congress Cataloging-in-Publication Data

Patterson, Jerry L.
   Casino gambling.
   Bibliography: p.
   1. Gambling systems. 2. Gambling. I. Title.
[GV1302.P37   1982b]   795   82-5230
ISBN 0-399-50656-X   AACR2

First Perigee edition: 1982

Printed in the United States of America

29   28   27   26   25   24   23   22   21   20   19

CONTENTS

Foreword

This book is written as a guide—for the novice as well as the experienced player—to the four most popular table games offered in today's casinos: craps, roulette, baccarat, and blackjack. The rules for each game are carefully explained and the text is illustrated so the reader can see for himself exactly how the games are played. The proper procedure for betting in each game is described in detail, showing where each bet is made, how it is handled by the dealer or croupier, and the manner in which winning wagers are paid.

The amateur gambler has three basic needs as he enters the casino. He needs to know:

- How to play the game in a sophisticated manner.
- How to exploit and capitalize on a short-term winning streak.
- How to minimize the casino's inexorable long-term advantage.

This book will address itself to these three needs.

1.

Evolution of a Gambler

The course of a typical player, from the point where he first becomes interested in gaming to the point where he either continues to play at a particular level or quits altogether, is easily charted:

- The novice is preoccupied with the fundamentals of the game—the basic rules and procedures.

- After some experience, the player becomes aware of the house percentages—the bets that are most favorable to the casino.

- The next stage is the grasping of rudimentary money management—bet sizes that will extend playing time.

- Confident with his acquired knowledge, the average player now begins his quest for the magic formula—the system that will overcome the inherent house advantage.

- Finally, the typical gamer will arrive at one of three stages.
  1. Disillusioned with his surefire systems—he quits!
  2. Convinced of the eventual success of his systems, he becomes a confirmed gambler—a loser!
  3. After thoroughly studying the game of his choice and establishing realistic expectations, he becomes a smart player—one who plays for pleasure, limits his losses, and capitalizes on the occasional big win.

The purpose of this book is to guide the reader through all these stages, avoiding disappointment, and explaining in detail how to become a smart player. A few people (less than 2%) eventually realize that counting cards at blackjack is the only sure way to overcome the house edge and take the steps necessary to become an investor—not a gambler.

2.

A Guided Tour Through the Casino

When you gamble in a casino, you should consider your gambling decisions as investment decisions. If you decided to purchase a stock, you would certainly take time to analyze the company and its products. Put forth the same effort prior to your next gambling trip, and you should reap a healthy return in terms of money saved (not lost) and money won. Your objectives in the casino are the same as in the stock market: minimize your losses and maximize your gains.

Test your knowledge of casino gambling games as investment decisions by answering the following questions:

- In roulette, as played in the Atlantic City casinos, which bets cut the casino advantage in half?

- In craps, which bet pays off at true odds (the casino makes no money from this bet)?

- In which casino game can you actually gain a small advantage?

- Do all slot machines drop the same percentage of the money played?

- What are the worst bets you can make (bets with the highest casino advantage)?

- What are the best bets you can make (bets with the lowest casino advantage)?

- Does the 5% commission charge on winning banker bets make bets on the player more favorable in baccarat?

Let's walk through a typical casino and find the answers to these questions. Thus armed, you will have a much better chance of winning the next time you visit one. In Atlantic City there are presently nine casinos open: Resorts International, Caesars Boardwalk Regency, Bally's Park Place, the Sands, Harrah's, Golden Nugget, Playboy, the Claridge's Hi-Ho, and the Tropicana.

They all have one thing in common. As you walk into the casino, you are confronted with a sea of slot machines and an incessant sound: a distinctive thud as the arm is pulled, followed by the whir of spinning wheels. This action is repeated in quick random succession so that the sound becomes a rhythmic blur in the background. Drop a coin in one and try it out. The result is immediately apparent in the machine's windows where you watch the wheels come to rest. You can drop nickels, quarters, half-dollars, and dollars into the slots, but go easy—they don't call them "one-armed bandits" for nothing. Seventeen percent of all the money played goes to the house. Perhaps we had better move on to a table game. Let's try roulette.

The favorite game in the more elegant European casinos, roulette is one of the least popular games in Atlantic City and Nevada because of the increased casino advantage with American rules. However, there's a major difference between roulette as it's played in Atlantic City and the roulette game offered by most of the Nevada casinos. A rule similar to the European rule called "en prison" has been incorporated into the Atlantic City game. This rule works with all the even-money bets: red-black, odd-even, high (19–36), and low (1–18). If either green zero comes up, you can surrender half your bet and retain the other half. This feature cuts the casino advantage on even-money bets in half—from 5.26 to 2.63%. Even better is the game offered in Playboy, with the single zero that reduces the house edge on all bets to 2.70%. These features make roulette an enjoyable experience for the occasional gambler.

Watch a few spins of the wheel before you place your bet. Notice that there are 36 numbers plus a zero and a double zero. Eighteen numbers are red, eighteen are black, and the zeros are green. Purchase chips from the croupier and place a $2 bet on the big red square at the bottom of the roulette betting layout. The croupier spins the wheel in one direction, the ball in the opposite. If the ball drops into any red number, you win $2, black you lose, green you surrender half your bet and the other half is returned to you. The bottom of the layout contains all the even-money bets. You can bet that a number between 1 and 18 will come up, an even number, a red number, an odd number, a black number, or a number between 19 and 36. If you stay at the wheel for a while, I suggest you stick with these even-money bets to keep the house's advantage to the minimum 2.63%.

Next let's step into the subdued elegance of the baccarat pit. Notice the deeper pile rugs, the richly upholstered armchairs, and the tuxedo-clad croupiers. The game and environment are quiet and calm in the European tradition. The game is easy enough to play and can be learned in a few minutes by examining any of the casino gaming guides. Only two simple decisions are required: how much to bet and whether to bet player or bank.

Baccarat is a game for high rollers. At the Atlantic City casinos, minimum bets range from $5 to $20, and at certain games the minimum bet is set as high as $100. Because of this, baccarat is not a popular game. Most casinos offer only a few tables that seat fifteen players each, but it's a good game to play because of the low house advantage: 1.06% net after a 5% commission charge if you bet with the bank, or 1.23% if you bet with the players.

Now saunter over the blackjack tables. The first thing you notice is that there are few empty seats. Blackjack is by far the most popular casino game, especially so in the Atlantic City casinos, where you will find some of the best blackjack rules in the world, and where it is sometimes difficult to get a seat at a $3 or $5 table. This popularity is due to blackjack's being the only game in which the player can actually get an edge over the casino.

Blackjack differs from other casino games in that your chances of winning any given hand depend on the cards remaining to be played. In roulette, each spin of the wheel is an independent event and does not depend on what happened in the past. If red comes up thirteen times in a row, the chances that red will come up on the next spin are still the same. In blackjack, your chances of winning are dependent, to a large extent, on the tens and aces remaining to be played—if the remaining deck is rich in tens and aces, your chances of winning increase. Employing a playing and betting strategy to take advantage of these favorable occurrences, you can gain up to a 1.5% advantage over the house.

Most players, however, do not take the time to understand the fundamentals of the game; thus they contribute to the casino's ever-increasing profit margins from the blackjack tables. The fundamentals are simple enough to learn. At the Atlantic City casinos you are dealt two cards face up. Only one of the dealer's two cards is exposed. This is called the up-card. The value of your hand is determined by adding up the face value of all your cards (picture cards count ten and aces count one or eleven). You win if your hand has a higher value than the dealer's or if he breaks (goes over twenty-one) and you don't. The dealer has an advantage over most players because they must decide whether to draw additional cards, called hitting, before he draws. If they break first, they lose no matter what the dealer does.

There are four decisions you can make after you are dealt your first two cards: split a pair, double down, hit, or stand. You can also take insurance if the dealer's upcard is an ace. The percentage plays for these five decisions have been worked out through millions of computer-played blackjack hands. Called the basic strategy, these plays are presented in detail in the chapter on blackjack.

"Winner! Winner! Front-line winner! Take the don'ts, pay the line, eight came easy. Coming out, same good shooter. Craps, eleven, any seven, whirl bets, horn bets, highs lows and yos, place your bets." "Let's go—throw a seven, shooter." What is all the shouting about? Amidst this excitement you see a cluster of players crowded around a large oblong table. It's craps, the most exciting of the casino games. You get more action at the craps table in five minutes than you can get at the roulette wheel in an hour. This is a game the high rollers play, but it is also fun for the $3 bettor.

Find a $3 craps table with some elbow room and watch the shooter roll the dice. Notice the pass line on the layout, one of the best bets, because the casino advantage is only about 1.4%. You are betting with the shooter, the player throwing the dice. When the stickman announces "come out roll," place a $3 bet on the pass line. A new series of rolls is starting. If the first roll is a 7 or 11, you immediately win your bet and collect $3. If the first roll is a 2, 3, or 12, you have lost your bet. If another number—4, 5, 6, 8, 9, or 10—is rolled, you have a point and the shooter keeps rolling until he either makes his point, in which case you win, or throws a 7, in which case the casino wins. When the shooter has established his point, you may take a free-odds (or backup) bet. This bet is usually no higher than your pass-line bet and is positioned directly behind it on the layout. Because it is the only bet in the casino that is paid off at true odds, it is never announced and there is no place for the bet marked off on the layout. With no house percentage the free odds on points 4 and 10 pay off at two to one; points 5 and 9 pay off at three to two; points 6 and 8 pay off at six to five.

Whatever game you select, play the best bets as listed below, stay away from the worst bets, and with a little luck, you may come out a winner. If you would like to depend on a little more than pure luck, study the game as it's explained in this book. If you are not familiar with these terms, you probably don't know enough about the game to play it.

Exhibit 1:

Best Bets

Game/Bet	% Casino Advantage
Blackjack/Counting Cards	−1.5 (Player has the advantage)
Blackjack/Basic strategy	0.4
Craps/Pass Line with Full Odds	0.85

Game/Bet	% Casino Advantage
Craps/Pass Line	1.41
Baccarat/Bank	1.06
Baccarat/Player	1.23
Roulette/Even-Money Bets—	
Double Zero	2.63
Roulette/All Bets—	
Single Zero	2.70

Worst Bets

Roulette/Inside Bets—	
Double Zero	5.26
5-number Bet	7.89
Craps/Field	5.26
Craps/Propositions	9–17
Slot Machines	11–17 (Less in Las Vegas)
Big Six Wheel	11–22

3.

Differences Between Atlantic City and Nevada Casinos

If you are a casino gamer who has gambled only in the state of Nevada, you have a number of surprises in store for you when you visit Atlantic City. Favorable rules make for some of the best games in the world. These rules, set by the state, are uniform in all the casinos; but if you are a high roller, you can't just walk up to a table, write a marker, and start playing immediately as you can in Nevada. You must wait for your marker to be cleared before the chips are issued to you.

This chapter examines Atlantic City casino gambling from two perspectives: the overall industry and the individual casinos themselves. We'll take a look at the major differences between the Atlantic City and Nevada gambling industry, and looking at each of the nine open casinos, we'll discuss some of their credit, "comps" (the term used for any sort of complimentary service—from drinks to a ride in a casino plane—provided by the casino), entertainment, and parking policies.

When Resorts International Hotel Casino opened its doors in May 1978, more than six months after the referendum passed which legalized gambling in Atlantic City, it was literally the only game in town. Casino gamers would line up two hours before the ten-A.M. opening to ensure getting a seat at the table of their choice. Demand was so great for seats at the $2 and $5 blackjack tables that people would crowd three deep behind them and contend with a two-hour or more wait just to get a seat.

In the peak summer season, lines of people would form outside the casino waiting to get in. The casino was often so jammed that there was literally no room for extra bodies. You had to fight crowds and squeeze between people just to make your way down the aisles separating the gaming tables.

From Resorts' management perspective these were indeed the halcyon days. A virtual monopoly on Atlantic City gambling for over a year pushed Resorts' stock from a low of five before the casino opened to a high of over two hundred. Resorts lost its monopoly in July 1979 with the opening of Caesars Boardwalk Regency. Now of course there are nine casino hotels open with several more in the planning stages.

The Atlantic City win figures are mind-boggling. In its first year, the Resorts Casino won about a third as much as all the casinos in Nevada. Atlantic City's nine open casinos are currently winning money at the rate of over a billion dollars per year. With the opening of the Tropicana, Atlantic City will probably win more than the entire state of Nevada won in 1982. Atlantic City's largest casinos average over half a million dollars in winnings per day—their percentages grind away at the thousands of people pouring through their doors every day of the week.

These heavy winnings are due to a number of factors which totally differentiate the Atlantic City casinos from their Nevada counterparts. First, size and proximity of market—sixty million people live within a day's drive of Atlantic City; second, size of casinos—with few exceptions, the Atlantic City casinos are huge football-field-sized rooms; third, access to casinos—gamers can easily commute by car or by bus.

It's this latter factor that characterizes the Atlantic City casino industry. Hundreds of buses pour into Atlantic City each day and disgorge their eager gamblers into the jaws of the casinos. These buses operate from New York City, Baltimore, Philadelphia, Harrisburg, and myriad other points in between. They are comfortable, cheap—actually almost free, because the riders get their fare back in rolls of coins, entertainment, or meal tokens—and have made Atlantic City into a "day tripper's" town.

There is one other unique factor that differentiates Atlantic City from Nevada and from any other present or future casino gambling area—the Boardwalk. Atlantic City's world-famous Boardwalk has been zoned for casinos. The distance from Resorts on the north to the Golden Nugget on the south is less than two miles, and within a few years nearly twenty casinos may operate along the five-mile length of the Boardwalk. The casino gambler can walk out of the door of one casino and be inside another in minutes. For those who are reluctant to walk, motorized trams make frequently scheduled runs up and down the entire Boardwalk.

This centralization is a tremendous advantage for Atlantic City. If they are losing, many players will change tables or casinos at the drop of a hat. If casinos are legalized in New York State, can you imagine driving to a casino in the Catskills, settling in, hitting a losing streak, and then having to walk back to your car and drive five or ten miles to change casinos? Not so in Atlantic City. This one factor provides Atlantic City with a tremendous competitive edge over any nearby state which may legalize casino gambling.

Even though the Las Vegas Strip casinos are next to each other, huge parking lots and busy streets make walking from one to another a tedious experience. You can walk between the Las Vegas downtown casinos, but gamers will come to prefer Atlantic City because the Boardwalk and the ocean provide a much more pleasant and enjoyable experience than downtown Fremont Street.

The casinos' overall management policies differ substantially from the Nevada casinos. Comps, while becoming more liberal in recent months due to increased competition, are still not as easy to come by as a comp in a typical Las Vegas Strip casino. You must be demonstrating substantial action at a $25 table in order to qualify for a comped dinner. Unless you are a regular, $5 action will get you nothing more than a comped parking ticket. Caesars Boardwalk Regency, as Nevada gambling veterans would probably guess, is the most liberal with its comps. Local high rollers enjoy their invitations to national sporting events shown on closed-circuit television in the Caesars showroom. RFB (room, food, and beverage) can be obtained fairly easily at the Boardwalk Regency and Bally's Park Place by showing $100 action at the quarter ($25) tables. I suspect that Resorts, which has had declining gross winnings, will now be liberalizing its comp policies.

Before the recent credit scam that bilked over $3 million from Caesars and Bally's, credit was fairly easy to obtain at the Atlantic City casinos. If you indicated a steady job and a bank reference on your credit application, you were almost home free. Now, credit is a little harder to come by, but it still can be obtained through the casinos. The use of credit cards to obtain cash advances in Atlantic City casinos has been ruled illegal. Certified checks can be cashed during weekdays at the cashier's office, but the cashier must verify the transaction with your bank. There is a local American Express office which will issue you traveler's checks provided you have the appropriate credit behind your American Express card.

Once you have established credit, the use of credit differs from the Nevada casinos. When you write a marker—which, incidentally, can be presented as a draft to your bank—the floor person accepting it must check your credit file before issuing you the chips. This can sometimes take exceedingly long minutes when you are waiting to get into action.

*　　*　　*

The Atlantic City casino parking policies leave much to be desired. It will cost you $8 to valet-park your car—more if you park overnight and leave your car in the garage beyond 8 o'clock the next morning. There are parking lots around some of the casinos and their rates are also high, $5 during the week and more on the weekends, depending on the season. Harrah's at present has the best parking: you park your car yourself in a free multistory connecting garage.

Resorts, offering both valet and self-parking, is a fortunate choice in that many independent parking lots are nearby. Caesars offers only valet parking, although there are two or three independent lots nearby. Parking is difficult at the Sands, Bally, Playboy, Tropicana, and the Golden Nugget, with valet parking only, and few independent parking lots in the vicinity.

The Atlantic City entertainment scene is bright. The same superstars that appear in Las Vegas casino showrooms are now part of the Atlantic City circuit, and cocktail lounges offer the same caliber entertainment as do those in Nevada. Although the New Jersey Casino Control Commission no longer requires each casino to offer showroom entertainment every night, this ruling has not cut down on the quality of the productions, or the variety. All that has been reduced is the frequency. Tickets to even the biggest name acts are available, and the prices are in line with Las Vegas.

Most of the big casino hotels are offering revues in their main showrooms as opposed to big-name entertainment. The big-name stars still shine in Atlantic City, but mainly during the "in-season" summer months. The cost of producing a revue is much less than paying the fat fees of the superstars. I personally prefer the lounge shows, especially at Resorts.

Atlantic City restaurants have improved markedly as the casinos continue to open, and they are beginning to resemble the finest restaurants in the big cities, presenting cuisines comparing favorably to the gourmet dining featured by many of the Las Vegas casinos. In this category, I especially recommend the Meadows at Harrah's, Playboy's Le Chat Noir, and Victoria's in the Golden Nugget. Prices are very high—$20-plus per plate, similar to high prices in the other casino gourmet restaurants—but the quality and the service are very, very good.

Resorts offers the best selection of restaurants, with a coffee shop and a deli located directly off the casino floor. Caesars offers the best buffet. The quality is good, and the selection is excellent. Especially good are the salads featured every day. Buffets offered by some other casinos, however, leave much to be desired. Although the prices are much higher than those in Las Vegas, the quality just doesn't measure up.

A hungry diner may do better by visiting one of the noncasino restaurants which are springing up, many of them located in neighborhoods very close to the casinos. Especially good is the Lighthouse Tavern, located in the inlet section on Pacific Avenue, about ten blocks north of Resorts. The prices are very reasonable, and the quality is excellent. Don't be afraid of the ghettolike appearance of the neighborhood; there is ample parking directly adjacent to the restaurant. If you visit the Lighthouse Tavern, be sure to order the house specialty—french-fried lobster tails. This is the only place you can get this delicious dish in Atlantic City.

All Atlantic City casino hotels divide neatly into two categories, the old renovated hotels and the hotels built new from the ground up. Resorts, Caesars, Bally's, and the Claridge are in the former category, while the Sands, Harrah's, Golden Nugget, Playboy, and Tropicana comprise the latter.

The Resorts casino is a football-field-shaped rectangle, very long and fairly narrow, with table games surrounded by slot machines on three sides and part of a fourth. This casino has been expanded several times, and now features two cocktail lounges within its confines. The Caesars Boardwalk Regency Casino, octagonal in shape, features a skylight with real daylight filtering through to the casino floor. Although large, the unusual shape gives one the feeling of more intimacy. Golden Nugget is by far the most elegant. Sporting a Victorian English motif, it reminds me of what an early San Francisco casino would have looked like had one this large been built. The blackjack tables have red felt covers which match patterned carpeting, and small chandeliers and mirrors dominate the ceiling. Railings and walls surrounding the casino exude a rich, gilded appearance. Dealers wear clothes reminiscent of this Gay Nineties period.

The Atlantic City casinos have not yet cultivated the Atlantic City gambler to the degree of their Las Vegas counterparts. They are still depending on the surrounding local base of some sixty million people within a day's drive away. But the number of junkets offered definitely is increasing. For example, a company called Atlantic City Group Services runs charter jets out of sixty eastern cities and Canada that brought in more than 750,000 passengers last year. This same firm brought in an equal number of gamblers on luxury super buses that each carry only twenty people. Over the past two years, Atlantic City Group Services also has delivered another 500,000 people to town by more conventional charter buses. If you're a gambler interested in a junket to Atlantic City, you should definitely give them a call. Their number is listed in the Philadelphia directory.

4.

Nontable Games

SLOT MACHINES

I am often asked why people play the slot machines against such a disadvantage, why slot machines earn more money for the house than any table game. I don't know. It seems some people are just attracted by the simplicity of a game with no complicated rules of play or betting strategies to learn. Others, drawn by the impersonal nature of the game, enjoy the interaction between a player and a machine. Still others play the slots simply to pass the time. A typical scene in every casino is the large number of retired people attracted by the one-armed bandits. Progressive machines that sometimes pay off tens of thousands for a quarter give these retirees a run for their money. Las Vegas has some machines featuring a 97% return—97 cents out of every dollar being returned to the players, leaving the casino an advantage of only 3%.

Contrary to popular belief, the casino's edge does not decrease the longer you play any given machine. I have seen players feed money into a slot for hours, waiting for a jackpot to hit, believing it's overdue. It just doesn't work that way. The three or four reels inside the machine could hit two jackpots in succession just as easily as going for hundreds of cycles with no jackpot at all. As hard as I try, I cannot convince my mother of this fact.

She lives in Las Vegas and is one of the many senior citizens mentioned earlier who enjoy playing the nickel slots. My mother has spent as much as eighteen hours playing a progressive machine waiting for the jackpot to hit, with my stepfather relieving her for food and bathroom breaks. She has pictures framed of her slot jackpots, some of which are over $1,000. Of course, she hasn't told me how much she invested to win these jackpots. She does admit, however, to plowing all her winnings back because she has such a good time.

Although this book does not address itself to slot machines or the other game with no rules to learn, the Wheel of Fortune, I realize that many people enjoy the hypnotic pleasure of pulling the handle back and forth and watching the symbols spin in the payoff windows, and I offer these tips for playing the slots. Some machines are set to pay more money than others. The legal minimum in New Jersey is 83%, but some machines will return 85 to 90% of all the money played as winnings. Watch the other players and see if you can find one. Ask around; the machine attendants and other players are often friendly, and they may point one out.

In some casinos, the machines nearest the doorway pay

off more jackpots; this is to entice the passersby to come on in and try their luck. With some machines, to get the higher drop, you have to play five coins at a time. Playing five coins in the Jennings machines at both Resorts and Caesars gives you more payoff combinations. You win more often, but you are risking more of your bankroll. If your bankroll is small, it will usually last longer, even with the smaller return, if you play one coin at a time. Only you can decide whether you want the action or the longer duration of play.

Almost all slot players lose a far greater portion of their bankroll than the 17% edge held by the house, because they add their winnings to their bank and keep right on playing until all or almost all of it is gone. If you have to play the slots, my money-management advice would be this: Buy as many rolls of coins as you are willing to risk, and as you play, put all the winnings in your pocket. When you lose the last coin in the last roll, quit! Over a period of time, you'll bring home 83% of the money you start with, by far a better result than the expectation of the average player. And who knows? From time to time, you might hit a jackpot and quit a big winner.

Slot-machine addicts will enjoy the new games offered by all of the Atlantic city casinos—video blackjack, draw poker, and progressive slot machines. Video blackjack is played on a slot-machine-like device with a TV screen showing the player's hand and the dealer's hand. The machine is programmed to deal from a 52-card deck shuffled after each game. The rules vary from casino to casino, and I would estimate the odds against the player in this game to be anywhere from 5 to 10%.

Golden Nugget offers the best video-blackjack game. The rules are as follows:

• The dealer stands on all 17's.

• Ties are returned to the player.

• Insurance pays two to one.

• Split any pair (split aces, take one card only).

• Double down on any two cards of 11 or less.

• All wins (including blackjack) pay one to one.

You may bet from $1 to $8 on the play of each hand. Card counters have no advantage, as the cards are shuffled after each hand.

Bally's, Hi-Ho, the Sands, and Resorts offer similar video-blackjack games, in which the house takes all ties except for blackjack, but blackjack pays three to two as opposed to even money. These games offer a six-card automatic winner, and you may double down on 10 and 11 only. Pair-split and insurance options are not available, and the loss of a tie makes this game less attractive than the one at the Golden Nugget. Playboy and Caesars offer a similar game, except with no pair-splitting or insurance options, and doubling on 10 and 11 only. They do return the ties to the player and automatically pay a six-card hand. All wins pay one to one.

Video draw poker is offered in all casinos, with slightly varying rules. Betting from $1 to $5, you can win as much as $5,000 on a royal flush (with a $5 bet). The best games are found at the Hi-Ho, the Sands, and again at the Golden Nugget. The table of payoffs is shown below:

Hand	Payoff per dollar bet
• Two pairs	$ 2
• Three of a kind	$ 3
• Straight	$ 5
• Flush	$ 7
• Full house	$ 10
• Four of a kind	$ 40
• Straight flush	$100
• Royal flush	$500

The payoffs shown are for each dollar bet except for the royal flush, which increases to $5,000 for a maximum bet of $5. Although its payoffs aren't quite as good as those listed above, Caesars probably offers the best odds because your bet is returned to you if your hand ends up as a pair of jacks or better.

Progressive slot machines are an outgrowth of the competition among the nine Atlantic City hotel casinos. Slot-machine devotees should check around for the highest payoffs available for the lowest bet, because they vary from week to week as the progressive jackpots are hit. On a recent visit, I found the highest jackpot for the lowest wager at the Hi-Ho Casino. Just three quarters (seventy-five cents) could win $40,000 on one machine, and

$34,000 on a second machine. On the other hand, the Hi-Ho offered a $10 machine where a wager of $3 could win only a total of $32,000. The highest payoffs are available at Resorts—a $3 wager could win as much as $150,000.

In most casinos it's very easy to find the progressive slot machines; merely look up on the wall and you'll see a digital readout of the amount of the progressive jackpot located right over the bank of machines. The casinos want to advertise these machines because they know that many players enjoy going for the very high payoffs. But be very choosy in your selection of a machine; I noticed some players dropping in dollars for a much smaller jackpot than they could get by playing quarters on a machine one or two rows away.

BIG SIX WHEEL

As you emerge from the slot area, you will notice a wheel rotating lazily around a central axle. This is the Big Six Wheel, or Wheel of Fortune, an even easier game to play than the slots. All you have to do is lay your money on the table. How do you go about it? The wheel contains 54 slots, each identified by a number—1, 2, 5, 10, 20, and a joker or casino logo. On the table in front of you are squares corresponding to the numbered slots, or lettered with the word "joker" or the casino name. You can bet a minimum of $1 on one or more of the betting squares, and if the wheel stops on your selection, you win.

Bet	Payoff	Casino Advantage
$ 1 slot	1 to 1	14.8%
$ 2 slot	2 to 1	16.7%
$ 5 slot	5 to 1	11.1%
$10 slot	10 to 1	18.5%
$20 slot	20 to 1	22.2%
Joker or Logo	45 to 1	14.8%

If you must play the Big Six Wheel, your best bet is the $5 slot, where you will lose your money half as fast as on the $20 slot, which is the worst bet.

5.

CRAPS

HISTORY

The casino game of craps, evolved over thousands of
years, is inextricably interwoven with the development of
humanity. Prehistoric cavemen cast six-sided bones called
astragalas that came from the ankles of clove-footed ani-
mals. The mythology of ancient Egypt, Greece, and
Rome relates how the gods amused themselves at dice,
with the destiny of the world riding on the outcome. Dice
have been found in the ruins of Pompeii and in the burial
chambers of the pyramids. The pharaohs as well as the
Caesars* rolled dice for amusement, gain, divination, and
judicial decision. When Julius Caesar defied the Roman

*Claudius (10 B.C.–A.D. 54), the grandson of Mark Antony (who had whiled
away odd moments at Alexandria engaging in dice games), was the author of a
book, *How to Win at Dice*, which, unfortunately, has not survived. (Richard A.
Epstein, *The Theory of Gambling and Statistical Logic*.)

Senate and led his victorious army across the Rubicon, he took his announcement from the vocabulary of the dice shooter: *Iacta alea est,* the die is cast. Even in the age of chivalry, knights entertained themselves and their ladies with games of dice. Gaming schools and guilds flourished, although by then gambling was frowned on by the church and was frequently prohibited. Then, as now, the nobility was exempted, and the laws were enforced against the lower classes, especially on working days.

Today's casino craps can be traced directly to the game of hazard, first played by English Crusaders during the siege of an Arabian castle in the twelfth century. Tosses of 2, 3, or 12 were referred to as "crabs." By the early 1800's, when the game was introduced to America in the port city of New Orleans, "crabs" had become "craps" and the rules had nearly evolved to those used today. Spreading rapidly up the Mississippi with the riverboat gamblers, and across the country via Pullman-car sharks, craps quickly replaced faro as the most popular gambling game. John H. Winn is credited with banking the first craps game permitting right and wrong betting, charging bettors a 5% commission. Shortly after, Winn designed the "Philadelphia Layout," very much like the craps layout of today, and included a don't-pass line which eventually developed into the Don't Pass Bar 12 line and eliminated the 5% commission. This feature took the game out of the streets and into the casinos.

TODAY'S GAME

Craps is my favorite game. You can yell and shout and let it all hang out. There is a camaraderie at the craps table found in no other casino game. Unlike blackjack, in which the cards are dealt by a dealer, or roulette, in which the croupier spins the wheel, in craps the player initiates the action by throwing the dice.

Although the house's edge can be reduced to less than one percent, it must prevail in the long run. Yet players who understand the rules and procedures of the game—which bets are most favorable, which bets to avoid, how to recognize and capitalize on a winning streak, and when to quit—can get a lot of fun and excitement for their money, and from time to time go home with a bundle.

Many people confess their complete ignorance of the casino game of craps. Some men, especially veterans, played a street game of dice which is quite different from bank craps as played in most casinos. In any case, the concept of craps is quite simple and easy to understand. The biggest problem in the casino is overcoming the idea that the game itself is complicated. Far from it; the stumbling blocks rest in the elaborate layout, the odds, the action, the barking of the stickmen, and the shouting of the players, especially during a hot hand. I will do my best to take away the bewilderment.

PLAYERS

Let's start with the players, men and women, rank beginners and old-timers, some laughing and shouting,
some quiet and grim. They are all ordinary people, just
like you and me. Most are playing for amusement, and,
win or lose, the game can be fun. Craps is not a group
game. All players bet against the house, and one player's
decisions in no way affect the others'. The number of
players is limited only by the number of people who can
squeeze around the table; so, if you can slip in sideways
and get to the layout, go to it.

We know if we are going to play we've got to bet, so we
will need chips, or checks. These colored disks are used
instead of cash for several reasons. First, the bankroll
needed by a casino is a fraction of what would be required if all tables were stocked with cash; second, the
different colors of the chips simplify the dealer's job of
paying winning bets; and finally, the possibility of theft is
reduced since stolen chips must be subsequently converted into cash.

Each craps table has a minimum-bet requirement. A
sign is positioned next to the dealers on either end to
indicate the table stakes. In Atlantic City, you can easily
tell the stakes by the color of the sign: white indicates a $2
or $3 minimum bet; red indicates a $5 minimum; green
indicates a $25 minimum; blue indicates a $50 minimum;
and black indicates a $100 minimum. Maximums usually
vary between $300 and $1,000, although top casinos will

raise the maximums at the request of a high-rolling player.

Place some of your currency in front of the dealer and, so that it will not be mistaken for a bet, announce clearly, "Change, please." Don't try to hand the dealer your money. Drop it on the table. Dealers are not allowed to take money out of your hand, and they are not permitted to hand you your chips. The dealer will usually repeat, "Change only," and hand the money to the boxman, who counts it and tells the dealer the amount. The dealer will then place the equivalent amount of chips on the table in front of you. Immediately place the chips you are not betting in the chip grooves provided in the table railing directly in front of you. Never leave chips on the layout, as they may be considered a bet. Remember that dealers must pay off all previous winning wagers and will usually set up new bets before stopping to make change. If you think the dice will be thrown before you get your chips, clearly announce the size and type of the wager you are making; if the dealer acknowledges it, called booking, you have a bet.

CASINO CREW

We have briefly mentioned a dealer and a boxman. They are part of a four- or five-man crew consisting of a stickman, two dealers, and one or two boxmen, who operate the game for the amusement of the players and the benefit of the house. The stickman, who conducts the

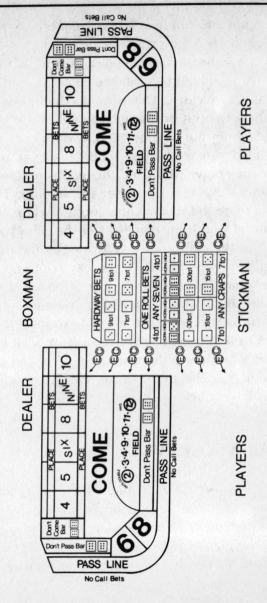

game, controls the dice with a hooked stick, hence his name. From a bowl in front of him, he pushes five or six dice to a player. If the player does not care to shoot, he points to the next player, who is then presented with the dice. The shooter selects any two, but when he is holding the dice, they must always be kept in view of the stick-man; if not, they will be called back and examined by the boxman, and the player will be offered new dice from the bowl. After the dice are thrown to the opposite end of the table, the result is announced by the stickman, usually ac-companied by a colorful banter. The stickman controls the pace of the game and also acts as a barker by calling out all the proposition bets that can be made with him. These are the worst bets for the player, the best bets for the house, and account for a substantial portion of the casino's winnings.

In addition to placing the "puck" on the shooter's num-ber, making change, collecting losing bets, and paying off winning bets, the two dealers, who stand opposite the stickman at each end of the table, are expected to help beginning players. Expert dealers soon become familiar with each player's betting style, anticipating their play and frequently correctly point out an overlooked bet. One or two boxmen, the ultimate authorities at the table, sit between the dealers, watching at all times the dice, the chips, the money, the dealers, and the players.

To eliminate any chance of the dice being controlled, the shooter is expected to toss the dice hard enough so they hit the backboard at the other end of the table. Thus control by the shooter becomes a near-impossibility when both dice bounce back from the embossed rubber-covered backboard. Although the throw is still considered legal if one or both dice fail to reach the end of the table, the boxman will strongly urge the shooter to throw harder. If a die bounces off the table or lands on a stack of chips or in the dice cup, the stickman announces, "No roll!" and the misthrown die is given to the boxman for scrutiny to prevent strange dice from being introduced into the game, while the remaining dice are offered to the shooter to select a replacement. No bets are won or lost, and players are free to change their wagers. If a die is cocked, or not lying flat, the stickman calls it the way the die would have come to rest, and the roll counts. Never let your hands get in the way of the thrown dice. If the dice hit your hand before coming to rest, it is considered an omen of bad luck. Many veteran craps shooters actually believe that this will cause a seven to be thrown and the shooter and the pass-line bettors to lose. Go along with this superstition—the dealers do. Listen for their admonition: "Watch your hands!" or "Hands up!"

TABLE AND LAYOUT

An understanding of the layout on the heavy wooden twelve-foot-by-three-and-a-half-foot table is the next order of business. The green baize cloth on the surface, a "Craps road map" if you like, permits the game to function efficiently. Of course we dare not do away with it, but if the layout suddenly disappeared, a dice game could still be carried on. But just imagine the dealers trying to remember all the bets some dozen or more players wish to make. The crew is very good, but they are not supermen.

Examine the two outside sections. Note that they are symmetrical, so a player can stand anywhere and have access to identical areas. The center section is under control of the stickman with his proposition bets.

I am always surprised by how many visitors to a casino play with real money without understanding the rules and conditions of the games. People who spend days comparison-shopping for everything they buy, from groceries to stocks and bonds, blithely toss their money on the table without the slightest idea of where the best and worst bets are. There are over thirty different bets on a craps layout, but fewer than half a dozen offer the odds that make craps the game with the best value in the casino, exceeded only by blackjack when played by very knowledgeable players. Let's make a study of the different bets with the idea of getting the most for our money.

COME-OUT ROLL

How do we start? Well, each player has designated spots on the table where his bets are to be placed, either by himself or by the dealer. Once you become familiar with the layout, it's a simple matter to locate and keep track of your bets. The stickman now announces, "The dice are coming out," and one of the players becomes the shooter. Players become eligible to shoot as the dice travel around the table in a clockwise direction, and when a new shooter takes the dice, all players make their bets. Because most gamblers bet on the pass line with the shooter, almost everyone at the table pulls for the shooter to "make his point" or throw his winning number before he throws a seven. In craps jargon, this is called "do" or "right"-side betting. "Don't"-side betting, on the Don't Pass Bar 12 line, is also referred to by many craps players as "wrong"-side betting.

PASS LINE

To shoot, you must make at least a minimum bet on the pass or don't-pass line. Both are shown on the layout. So when the cubes are pushed in front of you, select two and place a wager on the pass line, called the front line by inveterate gamblers, and throw the dice toward the far end of the table. When they come to rest, the numbers appearing skyward are added together and the total is called out by the stickman. The results of the initial throw, called the come-out roll, affect your wagers as well as those of all the other players, since some bets can be won or lost on the first roll.

If the spots on the dice add up to 7 or 11 on the first throw—a natural—the shooter and do bettors win; the don't bettors lose. This is called a pass and the shooter makes a new bet and continues. Should the initial throw total 2, 3, or 12—craps—called a miss, the shooter and do bettors lose; don't bettors win and the shooter does not relinquish the dice, but makes another bet and comes out with a new roll. When the total of the come-out roll is 4,

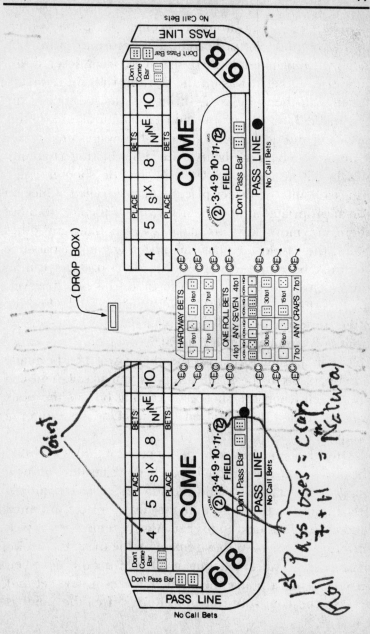

5, 6, 8, 9, or 10, this number becomes the shooter's point
and the number must be repeated before throwing a 7.
After a point is established, a roll of 7 is a loser rather
than the winner it was on the starting roll. All numbers,
other than the point or 7, thrown in the meanwhile (including 2, 3, or 12—craps—and 11, a natural) are waiting
numbers and do not alter the pass-line wager in any way.
Waiting numbers can be used for other betting situations,
which will be discussed later. When the shooter establishes a point, the dealer places a marker called a puck on
the appropriate number near the top of the layout. Since
there are more ways to make a seven than any other
point, the casino now has the advantage and a pass-line
bet can't be removed, although a don't-pass bet can. A
don't bettor would be foolish to cancel his bet, however,
as the odds now favor him. Never make a pass-line bet
after the come-out roll, since you have lost the opportunity of winning with a natural 7 or 11 on the opening
roll. For a similar reason, the house will not permit a
don't-pass bet to be made after the initial roll. You can
always tell when the shooter is coming out, as the puck
will be resting on the Don't Come Line instead of a
number.

After the come-out roll, the shooter continues to throw
the dice until a decision is reached, regardless of how
many rolls it takes. Should the shooter roll his point, he
and the do bettors win, and the dealer places an equal
amount of chips next to his bet. Always remember to pick
up your winnings—if they remain on the table, the dealer
may assume you are letting it all ride on the next bet.
After making a point, the shooter makes a new bet and
repeats the come-out-roll procedure. After the point is

established, if a seven should be rolled, the dealer whisks up the bet with great speed and without a "thank you." The dice now pass to the player on the left of the former shooter and it becomes his turn to shoot.

The pass line is the most popular area on the layout, and it's where some 80 or 90% of all players, mostly due to habit and tradition, make their wagers. The percentage for the house, only 1.41%, makes the pass line one of the best bets in the entire casino. Compare this with the slot machines, which are programmed to take approximately 17% of all the money deposited in them.

DON'T PASS BAR 12

Betting the don't-pass line, often called the back line, is just the opposite of betting the pass line, and is preferred by many veteran gamblers. The bet is made on the section of the layout marked Don't Pass Bar 12, and you are betting against the shooter, which could be yourself. Now the appearance of a natural 7 or 11 on the come-out toss will cause you to lose immediately. But when the cubes dance and come to rest exhibiting a 2 or 3 on top, you will experience the thrill of a win, which pays even money. However, craps 12 is a standoff. Neither the casino nor the don't bettor wins, and the gambler is free to remove his don't-pass if he chooses. It is this remarkable piece of arithmetic which permits the casino to bank all bets whether one wagers with or against the dice.

The house, as you recall, enjoys a positive expectation of 1.41% on the pass line, and through the expediency of barring the 12 on the don't-pass line, the casino realizes an advantage of 1.40%. Thus, one may stake on either line.

When the shooter rolls a point and then misses out, you win. If he makes his point, you lose. We have learned that most people wager on the pass line. Perhaps only 10% are wrong bettors, possibly because of the pessimistic connotation. It's unnatural for most gamblers not to be able to call with the other bettors for a natural on the come-out roll and for a steady stream of passes. Nevertheless, don't pass is not an erroneous or poor bet; on the contrary, it is one of the best bets in the casino.

COME BETS

If you really want to savor the action at the craps table, the come bet is the way to go. The come bet, made only after a point is established, is exactly the same as a pass-line bet except you can bet the come anytime you want—not just on a come-out roll. Let's say that the shooter has established his point, and he has thrown the dice two or three times and has still not made it. On average, it takes about three and a half rolls to effect a decision and, anxious for action, you bet the come by placing your chips directly in front of you in the come line of the layout. The very next roll of the dice establishes this new bet. If the shooter throws a 4, 5, 6, 8, 9, or 10, the stickman moves your bet to a specific spot in the appropriate number box on the layout, which indicates that it's your bet. As with a pass-line bet, a come bet cannot be taken down. Of course, if the roll had been 2, 3, or 12, your come bet would have been a loser. An 11 would have won. A come-out roll of 7 would have been a winner, but the pass-line bet would lose. With a come bet in the number box, you

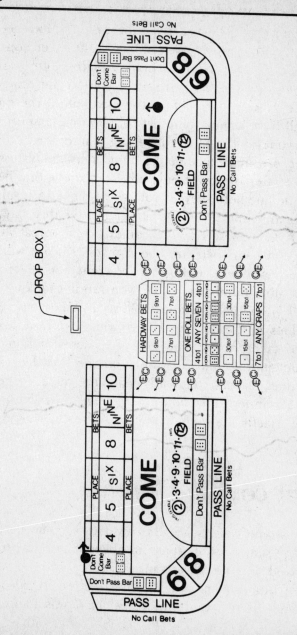

are pulling for the shooter to repeat the number before a 7. If he does, you win even money; if he sevens out, you lose. When you win, the stickman places your winnings plus your original bet in front of you on the come line. Be sure to pick it up before the next roll of the dice or you will have a new come bet for the total amount.

Everyone at the table, including a new arrival or the shooter, can make a come bet on all subsequent tosses of the dice after the come-out roll. It's obvious that betting the come line before every roll of the dice can result in a very exciting and profitable situation if the dice stay away from 7. Of course the 7 becomes a real threat after a number of come bets have been made, since it will wipe out the pass line as well as all the come bets. Even after the pass-line number is made, you are not looking for a natural 7 on the come-out roll, as it wipes out all the come bets in the number boxes, which we have learned can't be taken down. The dreaded 7 loses most of your bets, but it represents a winner on the final bet on the come line. Players frequently leave the table, forgetting this last winner. The house advantage on come bets is 1.41%, exactly the same as the pass-line bet.

DON'T COME

Don't-come wagers are the reverse of come bets and work the same as don't-pass-line bets. These wagers are positioned by the player in the space on the layout marked Don't Come Bar 12. The very next roll of the dice dictates the disposition of this bet. Craps 2 and 3 are winners and pay even money. Winnings are paid off on the don't-come bar, and if not picked up are added to the original bet, and the total becomes a new don't-come bet. As with the don't pass, 12 is a standoff and the bet can be canceled at the gambler's whim. A throw of 7 or 11 is a loser. Naturally, 4, 5, 6, 8, 9, or 10 becomes a don't-come number, and the dealer will move the wager to your designated spot in the appropriate box on the layout. Again, the venturesome don't bettor may make a series of these bets, but unlike come bets, these wagers are lost one at a time and the big 7 can result in the winning of six bets. The casino's edge on don't come is the same 1.40% as don't pass.

PLACE BETS

Place bets are by far the most popular number bets and resemble come bets in that you are betting on a particular number to be thrown before the 7. The difference is that your money goes right to the number instead of to the come line. Thus, if you put a bet on the table and announce to the dealer, "Place the 5," your chips are put on your designated spot in the place-5 box on the layout. If 5 is thrown before 7, you win and are paid off at 7-to-5 odds. The dealer will place your winnings in front of you and ask, "Same bet?" You can say, "Yes," and let the bet ride; or, "Take it down," and your bet will be returned; or, "Press it," and enough of your winnings will be taken to double your bet. Your odds on this bet are not very good—the house advantage is 4%. If you place the 9, the

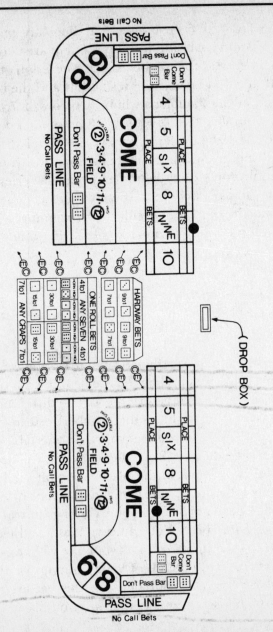

house advantage is the same 4%. Placing the numbers 4 and 10 are even worse, yielding the casino 6.67%. A place bet on the 6 or 8 is a completely different matter; the casino advantage of 1.52% is just slightly more than the 1.41% for come bets. Aggressive come bettors, eager for action, sometimes place the 6 and 8 right after the come-out roll, replacing the wager with a come bet if the number comes up. You must make place bets in increments of $6 to take full advantage of the odds when you place the 6 or 8. If you insist on placing 4, 5, 9, or 10, you must bet in increments of $5. If you bet less, you will be paid even money. If you bet more, you will be paid the odds on the next lower amount. Incidentally, place bettors of the 4 and 10 would reduce the casino's advantage from 6.67% to 4.76%, if they would buy instead of placing the bet. This requires betting in increments of $20 and is described in the next section.

Many craps players believe that place betting gives them a better deal, and the house less of an advantage, than come betting. This is not true. Come betting gives the house a small advantage of 1.41% as compared to place-betting advantages ranging from 1.52% to 6.67%. Why the large difference? Because when you make a come bet, you have a chance for an immediate winner when a natural 7 or 11 is thrown. It's true that you also lose immediately when craps 2, 3, or 12 is rolled, but this occurs only half as often.

Some players like to have all the numbers working for them immediately. "$32 across the board," means place $5 on each of the numbers 4, 5, 9, and 10, and $6 on the 6 and 8. The 4 and 10 pay off at 9 to 5; the 5 and 9 pay off at 7 to 5; and the 6 and 8 pay off at 7 to 6. Thus for every number the shooter rolls, the place bettor has a winner. The come bettor must wait for a number to be rolled twice before he can win—once to establish his point and the second time to win. Place betting in this manner can be very dangerous to your bankroll. In addition to giving the casino a much higher advantage, five numbers must be rolled before you recoup your investment. A 7 thrown early in the series will wipe out your $32 bet with little, if any, return. I have seen many players walk up to a table and say, "$32 across the board," only to have a 7 on the very next roll wipe out their entire bet. In come betting, your entire investment is not risked all at once. Also, a 7-out early in the series is a winner for you; 7 is a winner for the last come bet.

Another argument that place bettors offer pertains to long runs. Most place bettors turn off their bets on the come-out roll. A place bet can be taken down at any time, and this is, essentially, what they are doing on the come-out roll. Thus, if the shooter throws a 7 on the come-out roll, the place bet is not lost. If their number is thrown, their bet isn't won either. The come bet can't be turned off on the come-out roll and is lost if a 7 pops up. The house caters to this superstition by automatically turning off all place bets on the come-out roll unless the dealer is specifically informed that the bets are working. The theory is that this is when the shooter is supposed to throw his 7's. Therefore, during a long run which includes some 7's on come-out rolls, the place bettor's progression keeps working, while the come bettor must start over again after the 7 is rolled. The smart craps player ignores this faulty reasoning, sticks to the pass line, and makes come bets to get on the numbers.

PLACE TO LOSE

Place to lose is the opposite bet of place to win and is available in very few casinos. This wager is not very popular since nearly 90% of dice players bet with the dice, and knowledgeable don't bettors wager on the don't-pass or don't-come line. You must bet $11 or multiples thereof to place the 4 or 10 to lose, and the house advantage is 3.03%. At least $8 must be put up to place the 5 or 9 to lose, and this gives the house a margin of 2.50%. The casino edge is reduced to just 1.82% when 6 or 8 is placed to lose, and the bet must be a multiple of $5.

BUY BETS

Buy bets are nearly the same as place bets inasmuch as you are betting a given number will appear before a 7. The only difference is in the way the bet is made and the casino advantage. This wager can be made at any time by placing chips totaling $20 or multiples thereof plus 5% on the table and announcing to the dealer the number you want to buy. Some casinos will accept buy bets of less than $20, but the full commission on the $20 must still be paid, thus increasing the casino advantage. The dealer deducts the casino's commission as he puts the wager in your designated spot in the appropriate number box, and

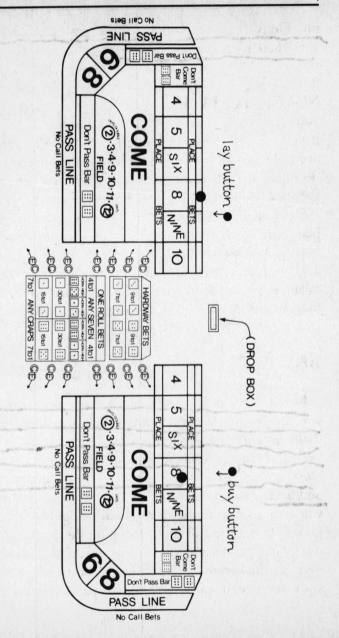

identifies it as a buy rather than a come bet with a small "buy" button placed on top of the stack of chips. If the number comes up, you win and are paid off at true odds, 2 to 1 for 4 or 10; 3 to 2 for 5 or 9; and 6 to 5 for 6 or 8. Now you must either take down your original bet with your winnings or pay the dealer another 5% commission if you want your bet to ride. Just like place bets, buy bets are automatically off on come-out rolls and can be taken down at any time. If you elect to take down the buy bet, the 5% commission is returned to you.

Since you must give the dealer $21 for every $20 you bet, the house advantage is 4.76% for all the numbers. Not only is this more than three times as much as the 1.41% edge for come bets, it is also worse than the 1.52% edge for the 6 and 8 place bets, not to mention the 4.0% margin on the 5 and 9 place bets.

LAY BETS

Lay bets are the reverse of buy bets, as you are betting a 7 will appear before a given number. These bets are made at true odds, 1 to 2 for 4 or 10; 2 to 3 for 5 or 9; and 5 to 6 for 6 or 8; with a 5% commission on the amount you would win rather than the amount bet, as with buy bets. The minimum lay bet is $40 on a 4 or 10, which yields the house 2.44%. $30 is required to lay the 5 or 9, and the house advantage is 3.23%. Oddly enough, the 6 and 8 are the worst lay bets, with a casino margin of 4.00% with a minimum wager of $24. Bets must be in even multiples or the house advantage is even greater.

FIELD BETS

A field bet, positioned by the player, is a one-roll bet. Unlike a pass-line bet, which occurs over a series of rolls, your field bet is won or lost on the next roll of the dice. This wager can be made at any time, and to the beginning craps player the field bet appears to be a really good bet. After all, you've covered seven of the eleven numbers; 3, 4, 9, 10, and 11 pay even money and the 2 and 12 pay double. You lose only if the 5, 6, 7, or 8 comes up. However, if you examine the number of combinations in which each number can be rolled, it turns out you would lose 20 units and win 18 for every 36 units wagered. This equates to a casino advantage of over 5%. The field bet is definitely not a good bet to make. You are much better off sticking to the pass and come line, where the house advantage is only 1.41%. If you insist on playing the field, find a casino, such as Caesars Boardwalk Regency in Atlantic City, that pays triple if a 12 is rolled instead of double, as at the other casinos. This reduces the house advantage to 2.70%.

PROPOSITION BETS

"Five dollars on any craps. O.K. Who wants the eleven? Ten on the hard four." The stickman at the craps table is like a circus barker, standing in the center of the table and controlling the flow of the game. His primary job is

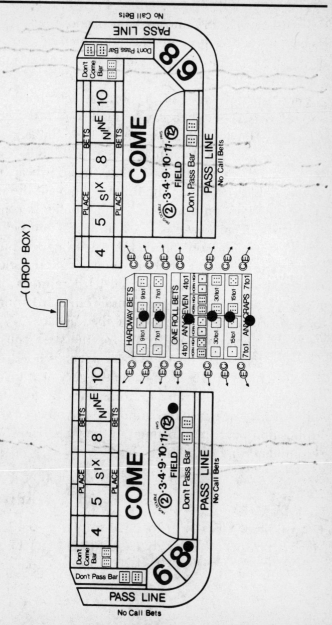

(DROP BOX)

to entice the players into making proposition bets. I call
them sucker bets because the odds against you and in
favor of the casino are extremely high: the casino edge
ranges from 9.09 to 16.67%.

There are two types of proposition bets: hardway and
one-roll bets. These bets can be made and taken down at
any time. Hardway bets pertain to the numbers 4, 6, 8,
and 10. A hard 4 is thrown as 2–2; a hard 6 is 3–3; a hard
8 is 4–4, and a hard 10 is 5–5. You win a hardway bet and
are paid off as shown on the following table if the shooter
makes the hard number before the number is rolled the
easy way (i.e., an easy 6 is a 5–1 or a 4–2) and before a 7
is thrown. When you make your hardway bet, put your
chips on the table and announce your bet to the stickman.
He will put your money on the hard number of your
choice, where it will remain until your hard number is
thrown or until you lose as described above.

One-roll bets are good only for the next roll of the
dice. For example, an Any Craps wager is a bet that either 2, 3, or 12 will be thrown on the very next toss of the
dice. You can make any of these bets by tossing your
chips to the stickman and announcing your bet verbally.
Proposition bets are explained in the table below. I don't
recommend any of them.

Bet	Casino Payoff	% Casino Advantage
Hard 6 or 8	9 to 1 (10 for 1)	9.09
Hard 4 or 10	7 to 1 (8 for 1)	11.11
Any 7	4 to 1 (5 for 1)	16.67

Bet	Casino Payoff	% Casino Advantage
2 or 12	30 to 1 (30 for 1)	13.90 (16.67)
3 or 11	15 to 1 (15 for 1)	11.11 (16.67)
Any Craps	7 to 1 (8 for 1)	11.11

Note the payoff column uses the words "to" and "for." 9 to 1 means that if you win, you are given nine units plus your original wager. 10 for 1 means exactly the same thing, but to the uninitiated it sounds like more. Beware of the casino that combines the two, *i.e.*, 15 for 1 for a 3 or 11 one-roll bet. Here the casino advantage jumps from 11.11 to 16.67%.

When you make a proposition bet and win, your original bet is not given back to you unless you ask for it. For example, if you bet $5 on the 11, you win $75 if an 11 is thrown on the next roll. Your $5 bet stays on the 11 for another roll. The stickman will usually announce, "Pay this gentleman $75 and you're still up to win, sir." If you don't want to bet on the next roll, you have to say, "Down with my 11 bet." This works the same way for the hardway bets. The amounts you may bet on the proposition bets are determined by the table minimums. At $2, $3, $5, or $10 tables, your minimum bet is $1 on any proposition bet. At a $25 table, $5 is the minimum proposition bet.

Many times you will hear a player call, "$1 on the yo," and throw a dollar chip to the stickman. What does "yo" mean? Eleven, believe it or not. This is the shortened version of "eee-ooo-eleven" which many players yell at the thrown dice if they have money riding on the eleven.

The C-E arrows around the Proposition Box in the center of the layout allow the stickman to keep track of all the popular Any Craps or Eleven bets around the table, as well as a combination bet called Crap-Eleven. This bet requires putting up at least double the proposition minimum and the chips are placed between the C and the E. However, one-half of the bet actually goes separately on each, and they are treated as two separate bets. If one part wins, the other part still loses.

To make a one-roll wager called a Hop Bet (the next hop of the dice), you toss the chips to the boxman, who places the bet on the table in front of him and just remembers it. The player must specify the exact combination of numbers coming up on the next roll. There are fifteen possible combinations made up of different numbers, such as 1-5, which is called Hop Ace Five or Sixteen, and winners are paid off at 15 to 1, the same as a one-roll 3 or 11. The six possible pairs are paid off at 30 to 1, the same as a one-roll 2 or 12. Hop Bets are available at very few casinos, probably because there is no spot for it on the layout, and the bet requires the attention of the very busy boxman.

Another one-roll bet that is rarely seen is the Whirl Bet. You must put up a bet equal to at least five proposition minimum bets, and you are covered for all the naturals, 7 and 11, and craps—2, 3 or 12. If a 2, 3, 11, or 12 comes up, it is paid off at the odds shown in the proposition box, and the other bets are lost. If a 7 comes up, the entire bet is a standoff. Of course, if any other number is thrown, everything is lost.

The Horn Bet covers the numbers 2, 3, 11, and 12. You bet four chips, each equal at least to the proposition minimum, and you are paid off for whichever of these numbers is thrown. Naturally, the other three chips are lost.

I must admit there is one proposition bet I do occasionally make—Any Craps. If I have progressed to a large bet on the pass line, I may want to protect it against a craps—2, 3, or 12—thrown on the come-out roll. I then bet what is commonly called "craps check," or enough money on Any Craps to protect my pass-line bet. For example, if I am betting $100 on the pass line, I lose if a craps is thrown. But a $14 bet on Any Craps returns me $98, a 7-to-1 payoff, and keeps my progression going. I now add two dollars to the $98 and make another $100 pass-line bet. I don't do this very often, as the 11.11% insurance premium is ruinous in the long run.

No longer available in Atlantic City, and to be avoided in other casinos, is the Big Six and the Big Eight, prominently located in the corners of most layouts. Big Six and/or Big Eight bets are positioned by the player, and win if the number appears before 7, paying even money. If you don't pick up your winnings and your original bet, it all rides on the next roll. The casino edge on this bet is a whopping 9.09%. If you want to bet on the 6 or 8, wager in multiples of $6 and "place" the number; then you will be paid at the rate of 7 to 6, decreasing the casino's advantage to 1.52%.

It has been said, "Casino games were never devised to favor the player." How true this is when, at the dice table, every bet has some percentage in favor of the house. So

far in our study of the layout, we have discussed some 30
possible wagers one can make. Well, the best betting
move is not even on the green. It's called the free odds,
or backup bet.

FREE ODDS

The first and foremost thing to remember is that this
bet is paid at the correct odds; therefore, you have an
even chance of winning. Thus, if the point number is 4
and the odds are taken, say, for $5, the house will pay
$10 for winning this 2-to-1 wager. But stop! Don't get
into the sedan or hop a bus just to take advantage of this.
Remember the house enjoys an edge on every play at the
table. You can take advantage of the free-odds bet only if
you have already made a wager on the pass line, don't
pass, come, or don't come. Of course, if you have a friend
who makes these bets and never takes the odds, you
could pick up a little action at no cost to you in vigorish
(the house advantage or charge taken on bets) by backing
up his bets with your money. Such players could be considered downright philanthropic, and if the casinos become aware of what you are doing, they will not permit it.

"Taking the odds" is the correct phrasing when a wager is made on the pass or come line. This bet is also
known as a "right bet," and the player is, or course, a
"right bettor." When a point is established—4, 5, 6, 8, 9,
or 10—the bet is backed up by placing the odds wager
directly behind the pass-line bet. Taking the odds on
pass- and come-line bets reduces the casino advantage
from 1.41 to .085%.

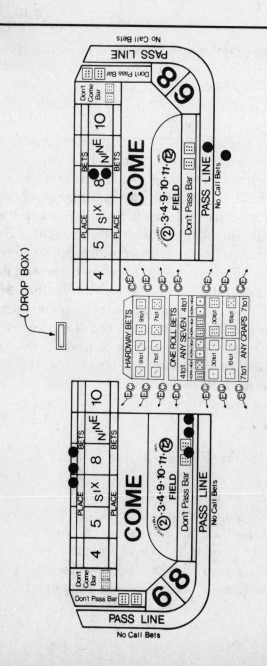

It is important to memorize the free odds so you can be
paid off at the maximum rate. Backup bets on 5 and 9
should be made in increments of two, so the bet can be
paid off at the rate of 3 to 2. The 6 and 8 should be
backed up in increments of five, so the bet can be paid off
at 6 to 5. The numbers 4 and 10 never become a problem, as the payoff rate is 2 to 1. In many casinos your
backup bet may not exceed the initial bet unless it's just a
small increase to make the payoff come out even. For instance, if your pass-line bet is $3, your backup bet would
be $4 if the come-out number is 5 or 9. With a come-out
number of 6 or 8, the minimum backup bet to receive a
6-to-5 payoff would be $5. Of course, the casino would
permit you to make a smaller backup bet than $5, but it
would be paid off at even money; the casino edge would
then leap to 9.09% on the odds bet. If the dealer will not
accept a larger backup bet, never increase the original
bet, which is always permitted. The increased original bet
would be paid off at even money, and the disadvantage
would not offset the gain of the odds bet.

MAXIMUM FREE ODDS

You can use this permissible increase in the backup bet
to gain a small additional advantage by betting in units of
3. For example, at the $2 table, bet $3 on the pass line. If
the point is 5 or 9, back up your pass-line bet with $4.
This bet pays you $6 if the shooter makes the point, plus
$3 for the pass-line bet. You are paid 3 to 2 for the odds

bet and even money on the line bet. Similarly, a $3 line bet would take a $5 backup bet if the point is 6 or 8. In this case, if the shooter made his point, your backup bet would be paid off at 6 to 5, yielding you $6 plus $3 for the even-money line bet. Using this strategy will further reduce the casino edge from 0.85 to 0.74%. The following table lists the increased backup bets that are accepted in most casinos. These are sometimes termed "maximum free odds."

Exhibit 2:
Maximum Free Odds

Line Bet	4 or 10	5 or 9	6 or 8
$ 3	$ 3	$ 4	$ 5
5	5	6	5
7	7	8	10
10	10	10	10
15	15	20	25
25	25	30	25
35	35	40	50
50	50	50	50
75	75	100	125
100	100	100	125
150	150	200	250
200	200	200	250
300	300	400	500
400	400	400	500
500	500	600	500
700	700	800	1000
1000	1000	1000	1000

When competition is intense, some casinos allow gamblers to take double free odds. If you have the choice, always play the casino offering double free odds if you are betting in this manner, as the casino edge is reduced to .061%. At the present time in Atlantic City, Playboy and Caesars are permitting double free odds and are also allowing an increase in the doubled backup bet to make the payoff bet come out even. Again, betting in units of three will maximize the additional advantage obtained by the double backup bets and further reduce the casino edge to 0.50.

Comparison of Casino Advantages

	%
Pass or come bet	1.41
Pass or come bet with free odds	0.85
Pass or come bet with maximum free odds	0.74
Pass or come bet with double free odds	0.61
Pass or come bet with maximum double free odds	0.50

The next table lists the increased double backup bets that are accepted in at least the two above-mentioned casinos. These could be called "maximum double free odds," and using this strategy will enable you to minimize the bet where the casino has the advantage—1.41% on the pass line—and maximize the bet where the casino has no advantage—the backup bet.

For those of you who make come bets, the odds and the procedure are the same as for pass-line bets. The only difference is that you place your free-odds wager in the come-line area of the layout after the number is established and you announce to the dealer, "Odds on the come number." The dealer will then set your odds wager on top and slightly forward of your come bet, which has been placed on the appropriate number. The odds bet is offset to indicate the two different payoffs. Watch your odds wagers closely and make sure the dealer positions them properly.

Exhibit 3:
Maximum Double Free Odds

Line Bet	4 or 10	5 or 9	6 or 8
$ 3	$ 6	$ 8	$ 10
5	10	10	10
7	14	16	20
10	20	20	20
15	30	40	50
25	50	60	50
35	70	80	100
50	100	100	100
75	150	200	250
100	200	200	250
150	300	400	500
200	400	400	500
300	600	800	1000
400	800	800	1000
500	1000	1000	1000
700	1400	1600	2000
1000	2000	2000	2000

Because the odds bets are free on pass- or come-line bets, they can be put up or taken down at any time, although for come bets they are automatically considered off on a new come-out roll. If the come-out number is a 7, your original come bets lose, but the odds bets are returned to you. If the new come-out number is the same as your come-bet number, you will be paid on the original wager, but the free-odds bet will just be returned to you unless you have announced to the dealer, "My odds work on the come-out roll," and he had placed an "on" button on top of one of your free-odds bets. This announcement must be repeated for each new come-out roll, and, of course, if a 7 subsequently pops up, your free-odds bet is lost and is not returned to you. Since a 7 is no more likely to come up after a point is made than at any other time, I always let the odds work.

Don't bettors can also take advantage of free-odds opportunities. The difference is that you lay the odds rather than take them. This means you put up a larger bet in order to win a smaller bet. For example, if the point is 4 and you have bet $5 on the Don't Pass Line, you are allowed to bet another $10, laying 2-to-1 true odds. If the 7 pops up, you win $5 on the first wager and another $5 on the second one. You have risked $10 to win $5 because the chances are 2 to 1 that a 7 will appear before a 4. Except for laying the odds instead of taking them, all the conditions for free-odds betting are the same for do and don't bettors, and the house advantage against the don't bettor declines in a pattern similar to the one for the do bettor.

Although the free-odds wager is the best bet in the casino for either the do or don't craps shooter, comparatively few dice players capitalize on it, including even those who are familiar with the mathematics. Nevertheless, if you confine your bets to pass or don't pass, come or don't come, always taking or laying maximum odds, you are giving yourself the best play for your money, and with some money management you are in a position to take a shot at the casino's bankroll.

MATHEMATICS OF CRAPS

Every gambler, whether occasional or serious, should have a basic understanding of the probability of winning or losing. This understanding is fundamental to maximizing your chances of winning against the casino. Walking into a casino without understanding the odds of winning or losing each bet you expect to make is the same as taking a job as a truck driver without knowing how to drive.

The key to understanding the mathematics of craps is knowing the frequency of appearance of the eleven possible total numbers—2, 3, 4, 5, 6, 7, 8, 9, 10, 11, and 12—that can appear when two dice are thrown. The following chart, taken from *The Facts of Craps,* by Walter I. Nolan, is the best illustration I've seen of precisely how 36 different combinations of the dice can produce these 11 numbers.

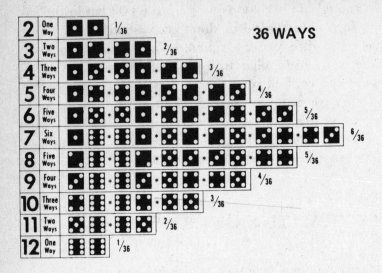

36 WAYS

Using this chart, it is easy to compute the true odds for any given situation. First, we determine the probability of each number being thrown. For example, there are 6 ways to roll a 7, according to our chart. That leaves 30 ways that a 7 will not show; therefore, the odds are 30 to 6, or 5 to 1, that you will not throw a 7 in one roll. Similarly, there is only one way to roll a 2, as compared to 35 ways to roll some other number; thus the odds are 35 to 1 that you will not throw a 2 in one roll. The next table shows the probability of each of the 11 possible numbers appearing on the next roll.

Now we can see the odds against throwing a natural 7 (5 to 1) or 11 (17 to 1); and a craps 3 (17 to 1), 2 or 12 (35 to 1). How about our chances of making a point number after it has been established? This can be determined by

	Odds Against
Point	Making
2 or 12	35 to 1
3 or 11	17 to 1
4 or 10	11 to 1
5 or 9	8 to 1
6 or 8	6⅕ to 1
7	5 to 1

comparing the number of ways the point can be made to the number of ways to roll a 7. For instance, if our point is 4, Nolan's probability chart shows it can be rolled 3 ways, as compared to the 6 ways to throw a 7. Therefore, the odds against making a 4 before a 7 are 6 to 3, or 2 to 1. By computing the true odds for every betting situation, and then comparing them with the payoff odds offered by the casinos, we can arrive at the precise casino advantage for every bet. The mathematics are not difficult, but they are tedious. The formulae are detailed in *The Casino Gambler's Guide,* by Allan N. Wilson and in *The Theory of Gambling and Statistical Logic,* by Richard A. Epstein. With the help of these two recognized leaders in the mathematics of gambling, we arrive at the chart on page 78.

Don't bother to memorize the percentages in this chart, since as a smart player you will be making only a few of these bets, studiously avoiding any wager with a casino edge approaching 2% or more. Making wagers which pay off with a disadvantage as great as almost all the bets on the chart is the quickest way to wipe out your bankroll. The only real difference between an astute craps shooter and a mark is the knowledge and use of percentages.

Exhibit 4:
Casino Advantage at Craps

Bet	True Odds	Payoff Odds	% Casino Advantage
Pass or Come*	251 to 244	1 to 1	1.414
with free odds			.848
with max. free odds			.740
with double odds			.606
with max. double odds			.500
Don't Pass or Don't Come*	976 to 949	1 to 1	1.402
with free odds			.832
with double free odds			.591
Place 4 or 10 to win	2 to 1	9 to 5	6.666
5 or 9	3 to 2	7 to 5	4.000
6 or 8*	6 to 5	7 to 6	1.515
Place 4 or 10 to lose	2 to 1	11 to 5	3.030
5 or 9	3 to 2	8 to 5	2.500
6 or 8	6 to 5	5 to 4	1.818
Buy 4 or 10	2 to 1	True odds less 5% of bet	4.761
5 or 9	3 to 2	True odds less 5% of bet	4.761
6 or 8	6 to 5	True odds less 5% of bet	4.761

Bet	True Odds	Payoff Odds	% Casino Advantage
Lay 4 or 10	2 to 1	True odds less 5% of payoff	2.439
5 or 9	3 to 2	True odds less 5% of payoff	3.225
6 or 8	6 to 5	True odds less 5% of payoff	4.000
Field	380 to 340	1 to 1, 2 to 1 on 2 and 12	5.263
Hardway 4 or 10	8 to 1	7 to 1	11.111
6 or 8	10 to 1	9 to 1	9.090
11 or 3	17 to 1	15 to 1	11.111
2 or 12	35 to 1	30 to 1	13.890
Any 7	5 to 1	4 to 1	16.666
Any Craps	8 to 1	7 to 1	11.111
Big Six or Big Eight	6 to 5	1 to 1	9.090

*Best Bets

Analysis of $3 unit bets at craps with maximum single odds

Point	Times Rolled	Total $ Bet w/odds	Potential Win $	Potential Loss $	% Win	% Loss	Total Bet $	Total Win $	Total Loss $
2	1	3		3		100.	3		3
3	2	3		6		100.	6		6
4	3	6	27	18	33.33	66.66	18	9	12
5	4	7	36	28	40.00	60.00	28	14.40	16.80
6	5	8	45	40	45.45	54.55	40	20.45	21.82
7	6	3	18		100.		18	18	
8	5	8	45	40	45.45	54.55	40	20.45	21.82
9	4	7	36	28	40.00	60.00	28	14.40	16.80
10	3	6	27	18	33.33	66.66	18	9	12
11	2	3	6		100.		6	6	
12	1	3		3		100	3		3
Totals	36						208	111.70	113.24

$113.24 loss, less $111.70 win, equals net loss of $1.54, divided by $208 bet equals a casino advantage of .7404%.

Analysis of $3 unit bets at craps with maximum double odds

Point	Times Rolled	Total $ Bet w/odds	Potential Win $	Potential Loss $	% Win	% Loss	Total Bet $	Total Win $	Total Loss $
2	1	3		3		100.	3		3
3	2	3		6		100.	6		6
4	3	9	45	27	33.33	66.66	27	15	18
5	4	11	60	44	40.00	60.00	44	24	26.40
6	5	13	75	65	45.45	54.55	65	34.09	35.46
7	6	3	18		100.		18	18	
8	5	13	75	65	45.45	54.55	65	34.09	35.46
9	4	11	60	44	40.00	60.00	44	24	26.40
10	3	9	45	27	33.33	66.66	27	15	18
11	2	3	6		100.		6	6	
12	1	3		3		100.	3		3
Totals	36						308	170.18	171.72

$171.72 loss, less $170.18 win, equals net loss of $1.54, divided by $308 bet equals a casino advantage of .5000%.

When you make a regular pass-line bet at the craps table, you are playing against a casino edge of 1.414%. To figure out exactly what this means to you, estimate the total amount of bets you might make in an hour and multiply it by this figure; the result will be an average hourly cost of shooting craps. For instance, if your bets total $1,000, the casino wins $14.14. This is in the long run. In the short run, which could be one hour, one day, one week, one month, or even one year, you may be on the winning side, or you may lose more or less than 1.414%. Every gambler walking into the casino believes he is the lucky one who will beat the house percentage. Sometimes you do, but more often you don't.

There are some astute craps shooters who call the lower casino advantage percentages for free odds an "illusion." Donald Schlesinger states:

> If two people each bet exactly the same amount on the pass line, but one takes the free odds while the other doesn't, they will both lose exactly the same amount of money (1.41% of the pass-line action) in the long run. The lower percentages above are always working on a *larger* bet than the player originally intended to make, thus the "illusion" of getting more for your money. In reality, when you stop to think of it, there is really no benefit at all where single or double odds are offered!

What I question about this reasoning is the phrase *"larger* bet than the player originally intended to make." I strongly believe that all bets, from the smallest to the largest, should be based on the player's bankroll and betting strategy; no bet should ever be larger than intended. Let's look at the following analysis of the action you can expect at the various types of craps games you can choose from.

Point	Times Rolled	No Odds	Single Odds	Maximum Single Odds	Double Odds	Maximum Double Odds
2	1	1	1	1	1	1
3	2	2	2	2	2	2
4	3	3	6	6	9	9
5	4	4	8	8.7	12	13
6	5	5	10	11.3	15	17.5
7	6	6	6	6	6	6
8	5	5	10	11.3	15	17.5
9	4	4	8	8.7	12	13
10	3	3	6	6	9	9
11	2	2	2	2	2	2
12	1	1	1	1	1	1
Average units bet in 36 rolls	36	36	60	64	84	91
Average unit bet size		$1.	$1.67	$1.78	$2.33	$2.53
Bank required to bet $5.93 per unit		$593	$990	$1056	$1382	$1500
$ per unit for $1500 bank		$2.53	$1.52	$1.42	$1.09	$1.

If you have a $1,500 bankroll and you bet three
units on the pass line at:

$1. per unit at a maximum-double-odds game, the
  casino advantage will be .500.

$1.09 per unit at a double-odds game, the casino ad-
  vantage will be .606.

$1.42 per unit at a maximum-single-odds game, the
  casino advantage will be .740.

$1.52 per unit at a single-odds game, the casino ad-
  vantage will be .848.

$2.53 per unit and take no odds, the casino advan-
  tage will be 1.414.

Since units of 3 are the most advantageous when taking
odds, round these figures off to a $3 base bet at the
double-odds game, a $5 base bet at the single-odds game,
and a $7 base bet if you do not take the odds. If, how-
ever, you do not vary your bet size for the same bank
according to the game you play, then the comments
above about the "illusion" of an advantage are correct.
The $1,500 bankroll used in this discussion is quite con-
servative, and, of course, you may use a smaller amount.
The important thing to remember is that you must vary
your bet sizes according to the type game you play for the
reduced casino advantage to be effective.

TYPES OF GAMBLERS

The craps table is the world in microcosm. You can
learn more about a person in five minutes at a craps table
than you can in a two-hour conversation. The next time

you play craps, watch your fellow players for a few minutes before you get too involved in the game yourself.

The "compulsive" player places all the numbers and has them working for him on every roll. He might start with "$32 across the board" or "$160 across the board." When a number hits, he presses the bet. For example, if 5 hits, he wins $7 but bets $5 more on the 5 and takes only $2 profit. If 5 hits again, he presses up to $15 or $20. If the shooter sevens out, the compulsive player comes right back with an across-the-board bet on the next shooter. The compulsive player must have action on every roll. He makes the wrong bet—place bets give up too high an advantage to the casino—and he overbets, by pressing up too much of his profits.

The "wrong" bettor bets with the house, on the Don't Pass. He lays the odds that the shooter will not make his point. If the shooter makes two or three passes in a row, the wrong bettor lays off and waits for the next shooter. Oftentimes, the wrong bettor is ignored or shunned by the other players. They don't like him because he bets against the shooter. But the wrong bettor is a smart player. He is playing near the casino minimum of about 0.8% advantage.

The "timid" player puts one chip on the pass line. You know he doesn't understand the game because he doesn't make an odds bet. He makes no come bets or any other bets. He patiently waits for the shooter to make his point or miss out. Other players may have won hundreds of dollars on a hot roll, but this doesn't faze the timid bettor. He happily picks up his single chip if the shooter makes his point.

The "high roller" is just the opposite of the timid

player. Many of the high rollers in Las Vegas are Texas oilmen wearing cowboy hats and fancy boots. They play with stacks of $100 chips, betting uncounted handfuls of chips on the pass line and come, and always taking the odds. They are a stickman's delight, as they love the proposition bets, frequently having one or more hardway bets going and usually responding with a quarter chip ($25) to the stickman's exhortation: "Who wants 11 or any craps?" High rollers enjoy the envious attention of the other players. They toke (tip) the dealers handsomely and are rewarded with lavish VIP treatment. High rollers would be smart players if they could learn to ignore the proposition bets.

The "analyzer" looks over each new shooter before deciding to "go with him" and how much to bet on the pass line. If the new shooter appears confident and has the look of a winner, the analyzer puts his money on the table. He makes a series of come or place bets. If the new shooter doesn't "look right," the analyzer reduces his pass-line bet and bets very conservatively. The analyzer frowns or curses when his "Mr. Winner" sevens out early in the roll.

The "grinder" is a hedge player who is attempting to eke out a small profit. He is playing against the law of averages and believes that, with his methodical betting procedure, he can beat the law of averages. The grinder makes a Don't Pass bet and then immediately places the same number. He collects a small profit if the number is thrown before a seven and breaks even on a seven out. The grinder loses fast when sevens or elevens are rolled on the come-out roll, but he may play for hours or even days before getting completely wiped out.

The "superstitious" player gets nervous when the shooter rolls the dice too hard and one flies off the table. He will turn his place bets and odds bets off for the next roll because he believes a seven always shows up after the dice fly off the table. The superstitious player gets very upset when the dice hit the hands of a late bettor or careless player. Again, this is when the seven turns up. He scolds the player who mentions the unmentionable seven during a long run because sure enough—on the next roll of the dice—a seven is thrown.

The smart player, or "tough" player as the pit bosses refer to him, commands respect and always is in control of the situation. Betting the pass line and always taking full odds, he also makes several come bets with full odds, betting up progressively as he wins his pass-line and come bets. If he is betting with $5 chips, he progresses from 5 to 8 to 10 to 15 to 20 to 25 to 35 to 50, etc. He never makes a proposition bet. On a busy or fast-moving table he watches all his bets like a hawk to ensure that the dealers make no mistakes.

What kind of player are you? I certainly hope you'll use this chapter to become a tough one!

6.

ROULETTE

HISTORY

Although the precise origin of roulette—the oldest casino game still in existence—appears to be lost in antiquity, there's ample evidence that men have gambled by spinning wheels for centuries. Ancient warriors whirled shields on the tips of their swords, and Romans turned over chariots to spin the wheels on their axles. The invention of roulette (from the French word *roue,* for "wheel") has been attributed variously to prehistoric Chinese, to French monks, to an Italian mathematician identified only as Don Pasquale, and to a brilliant seventeenth-century French scientist, Blaise Pascal, who at the age of nineteen invented and constructed the world's first calculating machine. In all likelihood, roulette simply evolved from other games of chance.

In 1765, roulette in its present form was introduced

into Paris through the efforts of a police official, Gabriel de Sartine, who wanted a gambling game that would thwart the cheats then plaguing the city. Its acceptance was almost instantaneous, and its popularity continues to this day. Just a little earlier, in 1739, a similar game called E-O (for even-odd), was first played in the city of Bath, England. However, the game became obsolete by about 1820, when refugees from the French Revolution introduced roulette, with its greater variety of bets.

Early-nineteenth-century roulette had both a single and double zero, very much like the wheels used in Las Vegas today. When the ball dropped into the red single 0, all bets on red were considered bars, and no money was won or lost. Conversely, when the ball landed in the black 00 pocket, all bets on black were barred. Interestingly, the same principle and terminology are used today in casino craps with its Don't Pass Bar 12 line.

The single-zero wheel, prevalent in Europe today, was introduced in 1842 by François and Louis Blanc, speculators in the French Bourse, who left France, where gambling had become illegal, to operate a casino in Hamburg, Bavaria. Their new wheel, which cut the house edge from 5.26 to 2.70%, decimated the competition, as the Blanc brothers had correctly forecast that reducing the odds would increase the attractiveness of the game and ultimately result in greater profits. After his brother died, François Blanc accepted an invitation from the Prince of Monaco, Charles III, for whom Monte Carlo was named, to purchase for nearly two million francs a franchise to operate his opulent new casino, where their roulette quickly became the most popular game, particularly with the elite. Gambling was still outlawed in France, and Monsieur Blanc, referred to as the "most brilliant financier of his time" by Lord Brougham, high chancellor of England, successfully financed the opposition to legalized casinos in Italy. François Blanc, who left a fortune of 200 million francs, and then his son Camille, expertly operated Monte Carlo for nearly sixty-five years and have been credited for its development into a world-famous resort.

Wealth and respectability did not come easily for François Blanc, as both he and his twin, Louis, served prison terms for stock fraud in France before achieving success in Hamburg. This scenario was repeated in the United States, where illegal gambling casinos had flourished since 1890 before becoming legal in Nevada forty years later. Many known gambling entrepreneurs with criminal records moved their illicit operations to Nevada, where their expanding businesses became legal and they became wealthy, law-abiding citizens. In the 1960's, large public corporations, led by Howard Hughes, began acquiring the major Nevada casinos, but until then many of them were still allegedly controlled by known criminals, and association with these same figures has prevented the licensing of several top management candidates in Atlantic City's casinos.

When roulette came to the United States through New Orleans in the early 1800's, the wheel in use had both the single and double zeros, but the operators, lacking the wisdom of the Blanc brothers, added rather than subtracted a zero. This third zero position featured a picture of an American eagle and tripled the house percentage over the single-zero game. Still not content, the operators speeded up the wheel to three times the pace of the leisurely 36 spins per hour of the game played in the European casinos. Undoubtedly, the greed of those early operators, still reflected by their successors in their stubborn retention of the double-zero wheel, is the cause of the relative unpopularity of roulette in American casinos that continues, unabated, to the present.

In the great gambling palaces of Europe, roulette is an elegant game. Played by princes and commoners, the very rich and the $2 bettor, it is steeped in a tradition that goes back to the eighteenth century. In Monte Carlo, the game is played in a regal atmosphere full of old-world charm. Many men wear tuxedos; women wear gowns. The vast casino, with its high ceilings and ornate chandeliers, has the appearance of a king's palace. Unlike Nevada casinos, there is little noise—just the hum of the spinning ivory ball as it circles the rotating wheel, the soft pings as the ball seeks the winning red or black numbered pocket, and the oohing and aahing of those who have chosen the lucky number. Already they are deciding where to place their next bets on the red-black-and-gold layout stenciled on the green baize cloth. Here, blackjack and craps are offered solely to cater to the whims of the American tourists. A large percentage of roulette patrons are women, who seem to appreciate the sophisticated environment of subdued glamour and relative simplicity of the game, although the action, in reality, is quite fast.

Roulette has never reached this level of acceptance in the United States. When legalized gambling first emerged in the thirties—and even in the preceding two or three decades when illegal gambling was available at posh spas from Saratoga, New York, to Palm Beach, Florida—roulette received more than its fair share of play. However, after World War II it was surpassed by craps, and subsequently both were eclipsed by blackjack.

Although casino gambling is expanding, roulette's share of the action continues to decline each year as consistently losing players become disillusioned with the game when they come to realize the inordinately high percentage they must face. Compare this to Europe, where roulette has been offered successfully for nearly 150 years. If roulette is ever to compete again with blackjack or craps, or even baccarat, the single-zero wheel with the European option of *en prison* or surrender must be adopted. Blackjack has become America's most popular and most profitable casino table game because players have learned that skillful play will reduce the house's edge to something less than 1%. Craps surpassed roulette because knowledgeable players, many of whom learned the game in the streets or in the army, knew that the basic bet, the Pass or Don't Pass Line, yielded the house a similar amount. As long as most casinos insist on maintaining their 5.26% edge, roulette play will continue to dwindle.

TODAY'S GAME

I enjoy roulette as a change of pace from the frenzy of the craps game or the intense concentration required of a counter at the blackjack table. There are a few single-zero games to be found, and there are some double-zero games that offer surrender, particularly in Atlantic City. In these games the casino advantage is cut in half, although the odds are still not as favorable as in Europe, where both single zero and *en prison* are offered. The knowledgeable player who understands the rules and procedures of roulette—which bets entail an acceptable risk and which bets are ruinous—can, with a little money management, get a lot of enjoyment from the game, and with a little luck can become a big winner.

PLAYERS

First we must purchase some special roulette chips. These can be obtained in stacks of twenty from the croupier with either money or regular casino chips, and they can't be used or exchanged anywhere else in the casino. Each table has its own supply of six or seven distinctly colored chips in sets of 300, one color for each player, and no one else can use this color until the player leaves the table. At this time he must surrender them for regular casino chips, which can be converted into currency at the cashier's station. These roulette chips have no monetary value printed on them. The buyer declares their value when he purchases them, and the croupier places a numbered marker on the table's supply to indicate their value, which can be any amount from fifty cents up to the table maximum. In actual practice they are rarely valued above $10, as regular casino chips may also be used for wagering. Since there is only one place on the roulette layout to make each bet, if another player has already placed his chips in a position you wish to bet, you simply place yours on top of his. Because of the different colors, the croupier can easily keep track of to whom they belong, eliminating any possible dispute between two players claiming the same bet. This American innovation is a distinct improvement over the European game, where there are frequent arguments over who placed which bet.

All roulette tables have two minimum bets, one for the even-money and 2-to-1 wagers, called the outside bets, and another for the number wagers, called the inside bets. For example, at a $5 table the minimum value of the colored chips would be $1 and one outside bet must be for at least five chips; other outside bets made at the same time can be for as little as one chip. Inside bets can also be for as little as one chip as long as the player has a total of at least five chips on the inside layout for the roll. There is no limit to the number of bets that can be made, although the casino does have a maximum limit for any single bet. This maximum is usually $100 for each inside bet, $500 for each 2-to-1 bet, and $1,000 for each even-money bet. Bigger casino operators will frequently raise these limits for high-rolling bettors.

Once you have a stack of chips and understand all about minimum bets, pick out a lucky number or spot, place some chips on the layout, and watch the ball spin around the turning wheel while you sit back and enjoy the aura of graciousness that surrounds the world's oldest casino game. When the ball stops, the croupier will mark the winning number, remove all the losing bets, and leave the winning wagers, which he then pays off. Players can now begin to make new bets, and may continue to place chips on the layout until a few seconds before the ball is about to drop, when the croupier announces, "No more bets." Any bets placed after this announcement are returned to the player, whether they win or lose.

CASINO CREW

The roulette game is usually operated by two croupiers. The one who spins the wheel and controls the game is sometimes called the wheel roller or, more frequently, the dealer. His primary job, in addition to selling chips and spinning the wheel in one direction while twirling the ball in another, is to announce termination of betting and the winning number, with its color, and collect all losing bets and pay off winning wagers. First he pays the outside bets, stacking the payoffs next to the original wagers; then he calculates the payoffs for the winning inside bets and slides them across the table to a spot directly in front of the lucky players, leaving the original wagers on the layout. Unless the players want the chips that remain on the layout to ride for the next spin of the wheel, they must remove them themselves.

The dealer's assistant, also called a croupier, separates and restacks, in the chip rack on the table's apron, all the losing chips that have been swept from the layout by the dealer. He also assists the dealer in paying off winning wagers by stacking the correct number of chips in a convenient spot on the left of the apron. All the larger casinos also have a pit boss who stands in the pit ring, watching the game, the croupiers, and the players. He handles players' requests for credit (called markers) and settles all disputes.

Inside Bets

Inside Bets

Inside Bets

Inside Bets

Inside Bets

Inside Bets

Inside Bets

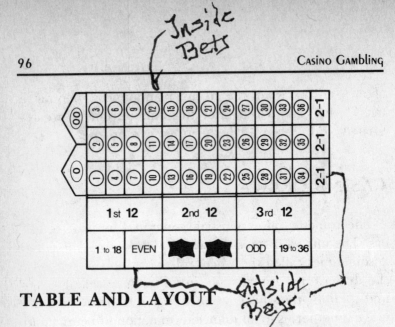

Inside Bets

TABLE AND LAYOUT *Outside Bets*

To the novice player, the layout looks formidable, but the game is really quite easy to learn. The main section is composed of 36 red and black boxes numbered in sequence from top to bottom and arranged in three columns of 12 spaces each. At the head of the columns, numbered 1, 2, and 3, are two more oddly shaped green spaces for the zeros. At the foot of these columns are three spaces marked "2 to 1." A bet placed in one of these indicates you are betting on all the numbers in the column above. Directly along the front side of the columns are three boxes marked "1st 12," "2nd 12," and "3rd 12." A bet placed in the first of these indicates you are betting on all the numbers 1 through 12, a bet in the second would cover 13 through 24, and in the third it would cover 25 through 36. Just in front of these three are six more spots for wagers on numbers 1 through 18, all even numbers, all red spots, all black spots, all odd numbers, and the numbers 19 through 36. You must be careful that your chips are placed precisely where you want to bet. If you can't reach a spot, slide your chips toward the dealer and tell him where to place them.

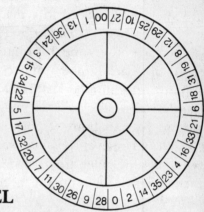

ROULETTE WHEEL

The game of roulette is based on a random choice of one of 38 numbers selected through the use of a wheel made up of a stationary 32-inch bowl which contains a precisely balanced rotating 24-inch center section called a wheel head. The ball is spun by the dealer in a clockwise direction around the outer rim of the bowl, and after circling a number of times, the whirling ball slowly drops down toward the center, frequently being randomly deflected by brass projections embedded in the rim. As it reaches the wheel head, which is turning in the opposite direction, the ball bounces around a number of times among the vertical partitions that separate the 38 numbered red, black, and green pockets before it finally settles in one of them, thereby selecting the winning number and color.

The 38 pockets, which are alternately colored red and black except for the green zeros, appear to be numbered in a random fashion, but that is not the case. As far as possible, high and low as well as odd and even numbers are alternately spaced in a mathematically balanced pattern. The single zero and the double zero are directly opposite each other, and 1 is opposite 2, 3 is opposite 4 and so forth. The numbers and colors on the wheel correspond to the numbers and colors on the layout. Understanding this, all you need now is an explanation of the various combinations of possible bets and their odds.

With only eleven possible wagers divided into just two types, betting rules are easily learned. First, let's consider the six inside bets on the numbers or combinations of numbers.

STRAIGHT-UP BET—Single Number

To make the single-number inside bet, simply place your chips in any one of the 38 number boxes, including the zeros, being careful that your bet does not touch any line. If the ball lands in the corresponding numbered pocket on the next spin, you win and the bank pays off at 35 to 1. Remember that your original bet stays on the layout and rides on the next spin unless you pick it up. True odds would have been 37 to 1; consequently, the house advantage is 5.26%. This edge is constant for all bets in the double-zero game, with the exception of the five-number bet covered below. When you find a single-zero game, the casino edge is reduced to 2.70%.

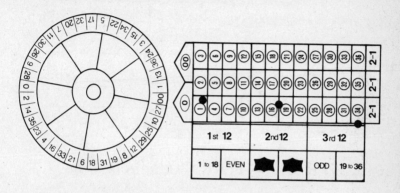

SPLIT BET—Two Numbers

If you want to bet on either of two adjoining numbers on the layout, put your wager directly on the line separating them. If one wins, you are paid off at 17 to 1. There are 62 possible two-number bets.

THREE-NUMBER BET

For a three-number bet, set your chip or chips on the line at the end of any of the twelve rows of three numbers; at the junction of the 0, 00, and 2 boxes; the 0, 1, and 2 boxes; or the 00, 2, and 3 boxes. This adds up to fifteen available three-number bets, and the payoff is 11 to 1.

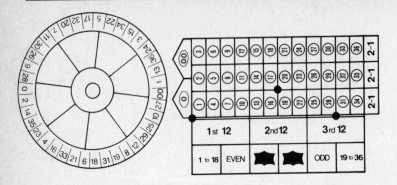

CORNER BET—Four Numbers

A chip placed at the intersection of any four numbers is called a corner bet. There are 22 of these, and if any one of the four numbers comes up, you are paid 8 to 1.

FIVE-NUMBER BET

The only possible five-number bet is on the line between the zeros and 1, 2, and 3 at the intersection with the 1st-12 box. Of course, this bet is not available in a single-zero game. In the double-zero game, it's the worst bet on the table, paying 6 to 1 with the casino advantage jumping to 7.89%.

SIX-NUMBER BET

You can make a six-number bet on the junction formed by the line dividing any two rows of three numbers where it intersects with the Dozen box. The bank pays 5 to 1 if you bet on one of these eleven combinations and any one of the six numbers is spun.

Next we'll explore the five outside bets, covering several groups of numbers, even-odd, and red-black, all spread over twelve betting boxes. These wagers still carry the same house edge of 5.26% for the double-zero game, and your original bet still is left on the layout after a win.

COLUMNS

When you place a bet in one of the three boxes at the bottom of the number columns, you are betting on all the numbers above it; if successful, you'll be paid at the 2-to-1 rate printed in these spots.

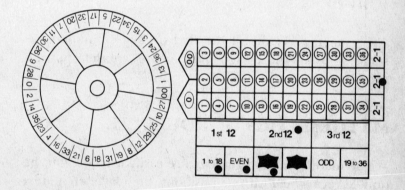

DOZENS

To wager on the first, second, or third dozen numbers, put your chips in one of the appropriate boxes. If any one of the twelve numbers within the dozen you've selected shows up, the bank also pays 2 to 1.

LOW AND HIGH NUMBERS

For a bet on all the eighteen low numbers or all the eighteen high numbers, merely set some chips in one of these two boxes to get even money if you win.

EVEN-ODD

Chips placed in either the Even or the Odd box cover all the eighteen corresponding numbers, and winners are again paid even money.

RED-BLACK

To make a bet on all the Red or Black numbers, set some chips in the designated box for another possible even-money payoff.

MATHEMATICS OF ROULETTE

The mathematics of roulette are easily learned. On the double-zero wheel with 38 positions, the player should be able to pick the winning number an average of once every 38 spins. Although the odds are 37 to 1 that you will select the right number in one spin, the payoff odds are only 35 to 1, and the casino edge derived from this difference of two units is 2/38, or 5.26%.

If you place a single bet on two numbers, you are in effect betting half on each number, and in the long run

38 spins of the wheel will produce two wins as compared to 36 losses. Therefore, true odds are 36 to 2, or 18 to 1, and as the casino pays 17 to 1, or 34 to 2, the house again comes up with the same two-unit-average advantage. The arithmetic is similar for all the inside bets except the five-number wager.

Unless surrender or *en prison* is offered, the outside even payoff wagers are not better. If you bet on the 18 red or 18 black numbers, the 18 even or 18 odd numbers, or the 18 high or 18 low numbers, you have 18 chances to win but the green zeros must be added to give you 20 chances to lose, and the house still ends up with a two-unit edge. With the three columns, and the three dozen bets, you have 12 ways to win, and including the zeros there are 26 ways to lose. The odds are 26 to 12 against you, but the payoff is only 2 to 1, or 24 to 12, once again yielding the casino the identical two units. Continuing with this formula, we arrive at the following chart.

Exhibit 5:
Casino Advantage at Roulette, Double Zero

Bet	True Odds	Payoff Odds	% Casino Advantage
Single Number	37 to 1	35 to 1	5.263
Two Numbers	36 to 2	17 to 1	5.263
Three Numbers	35 to 3	11 to 1	5.263
Four Numbers	34 to 4	8 to 1	5.263
Five Numbers	33 to 5	6 to 1	7.895
Six Numbers	32 to 6	5 to 1	5.263
Columns	26 to 12	2 to 1	5.263
Dozens	26 to 12	2 to 1	5.263

Bet	True Odds	Payoff Odds	% Casino Advantage
High or Low	20 to 18	1 to 1	5.263
Even or Odd	20 to 18	1 to 1	5.263
Red or Black	20 to 18	1 to 1	5.263

SURRENDER

The New Jersey Control Commission Rules of the Games state, "If the roulette ball comes to rest around the wheel in a compartment marked zero (0) or double zero (00), wagers on red, black, odd, even, 1 to 18, and 19 to 36 shall not be lost, but each player having such a wager shall surrender half the amount on such bet and remove the remaining half." This rule cuts the casino advantage in half, from 5.26% to 2.63% on all the even money bets, giving the same result as the European *en prison* rule, where the outcome on all even-money bets after the appearance of a zero is determined by the following spin. Atlantic City casinos are the only gambling houses in the United States offering the gaming public this feature, although I'm not sure if "offering" is the best word, since the state law requires it.

Bet	True Odds	Payoff Odds	% Casino Advantage
High or Low	*19 to 18	1 to 1	2.632
Even or Odd	19 to 18	1 to 1	2.632
Red or Black	19 to 18	1 to 1	2.632

*18 losses, 18 wins, 2 surrenders (one additional bet out of 38 lost)

SINGLE-ZERO GAME

An even better game being offered at the Playboy Casino features roulette with a single zero. Unfortunately, the surrender rule does not apply, but even so, the casino advantage is reduced to 2.70%, not just for even-money bets but for all wagers, inside and outside. True, the game is not as favorable as correct play at blackjack or the line bets in craps, but for the gamer who likes to play roulette, it's acceptable. The only thing I can't understand is why anyone in Atlantic City but the even-money-bet players would patronize the double-zero wheels.

Now that you are familiar with the rules and procedure of the game, and understand how to bet with the very least disadvantage, you must consider that in the long run your hourly cost will be a little more than 2½ percent of the average total amount of money you place on the table in an hour in Atlantic City. Only you can decide how much you are willing to pay for the pleasure of playing this exciting game. Of course, with intelligent money management you can control your losses. And who knows? You may come up a big winner.

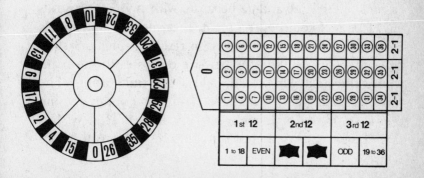

Exhibit 6:
Casino Advantage at Roulette, Single Zero

Bet	True Odds	Payoff Odds	% Casino Advantage
Single Number	36 to 1	35 to 1	2.70
Two Numbers	35 to 2	17 to 1	2.70
Three Numbers	34 to 3	11 to 1	2.70
Four Numbers	33 to 4	8 to 1	2.70
Six Numbers	31 to 6	5 to 1	2.70
Columns	25 to 12	2 to 1	2.70
Dozens	25 to 12	2 to 1	2.70
High or Low	19 to 18	1 to 1	2.70
Even or Odd	19 to 18	1 to 1	2.70
Red or Black	19 to 18	1 to 1	2.70

LEARNING THE HARD WAY

I remember my first trip to Las Vegas. Fresh out of college, and armed with an "unbeatable" roulette system, I came to conquer the casinos. I didn't care about the casinos' 5.26% advantage because, with my betting strategy, I knew I could overcome it. I was using a Martingale System and betting exclusively on red. Martingale System rules involve doubling the bet size on losses to the point where the next win would yield a one-unit profit. (The term "Martingale" originated from a London casino operator of the eighteenth-century named Henry Martingale who was always encouraging his patrons to "double up and catch up.") The first day, all went according to plan. The system was working beautifully. At one point, I had almost doubled my $100 bankroll. Then I hit a string of losses. My system was based on the fact that I would not lose nine times in succession. The odds against this were one in 512, so I figured I was safe. If it did happen, however, I was wiped out.

I sat at the table and watched black come up five times in a row. I dutifully increased my bet on red. Black again. By this time I was very nervous but I still bet red according to the system rules. The croupier spun the ball; mentally, I was trying to influence the outcome by "willing" red to occur. Black again. Now beads of sweat were breaking out on my forehead, but I was bound and determined to see this thing through. I pushed almost half of my remaining chips to the red. To no avail. It was almost as if fate was conspiring against me. Now all my chips were on the table. By this time I had lost all of my confidence and knew I was going to lose. I did.

The train ride back to Los Angeles was long and filled with hunger pangs. I had even lost my dinner money. The lesson in this tale is that it is impossible to overcome a casino advantage, no matter what betting strategy you employ. You may get lucky and win on one trip or many trips in succession. But in the long run, the casino advantage will prevail.

7.

BACCARAT

HISTORY

The English word "card" stems from the Greek term for paper, but actually, card games go back over 2,000 years, centuries before paper was invented. Historians have been unable to pinpoint their precise origins, but they have uncovered records of card playing in ancient China, India, and Egypt.

Like dice, cards were brought back to Europe in the fourteenth century by the Crusaders, and although the church was soon preaching that they were the invention of the devil himself, Johann Gutenberg printed playing cards in 1440, the same year he printed his famous Bible. Consisting of 78 cards, the pack was called Tarots, from which the modern deck evolved, with the four suits representing the four classes of feudal society. The nobility was symbolized by swords, in Spanish *espadas*, from which we get spades. Merchants were represented by coins, frequently square in shape, which, when turned on end, became today's diamonds. The sign for the serfs was literally a club, then called a baton, and today the cloverleaf-shaped sign is still called a club. The emblem for the church was the grail, or chalice, and from its characteristic shape developed our hearts.

Gutenberg's Tarot deck consisted of 22 "atouts," or trumps—including a joker—and four suits of 14 cards, each with ten numbered cards plus a king, a queen, a knight, and a valet or jester. Before 1500, the 22 "atouts" and the valet were dropped, although today in some games the five top-ranked cards are still called trumps, and in other games the joker (jester) is still used. Originally, the face cards were portrayals of actual personages, and slight traces of them remain to this day. Charlemagne was the model for the king of hearts; the Hebrew King David was portrayed by the king of spades; Julius Caesar was represented by the king of diamonds; and Alexander the Great was the prototype for the king of clubs. On the feminine side were Helen of Troy as the queen of hearts, Palas Athena as the queen of spades, and the biblical Rachel as the queen of diamonds. Also honored from time to time were Joan of Arc and Elizabeth I, as well as a number of others. The knights, or jacks as they came to be called, were all patterned after famous soldiers, such as Sir Lancelot for clubs; Charlemagne's nephew Roland for diamonds; Hogier Le Danois, another Charlemagne lieutenant, for spades; and Etienne de Vignoles, who fought for Charles VII of France, for hearts. By 1492 the modern deck of cards as we know it had been established and was introduced to America by Christopher Columbus and his sailors.

At about the same time, the forerunner of our present day baccarat made its first appearance. I am indebted to Richard A. Epstein and his classic work, *The Theory of Gambling and Statistical Logic,* from which the following is excerpted:

Introduced into France from Italy during the reign of Charles VIII (ca. 1490), the game was apparently devised by a gambler named Felix Falguiere who based it on the old Etruscan ritualism of the "Nine Gods." According to legend, twenty-six centuries ago in "The Temple of Golden Hair" in Etruscan Rome, the "Nine Gods" prayed standing on their toes to a golden-tressed virgin who cast a *novem dare* (nine-sided die) at their feet. If her throw was 8 or 9, she was crowned a priestess. If she threw a 6 or 7, she was disqualified from further religious office and her vestal status was summarily transmuted. And if her cast was 5 or under, she walked gracefully into the sea. Baccarat was designed with a similar partition (albeit with less dramatic payoffs) of the numbers, modulo 10.

Unfortunately, today it's the casino patrons who are usually destined to face a fate similar to that suffered by the would-be priestess when she cast a 6 or 7.

European baccarat (pronounced ba-ka-ra with soft a's and a silent t), baccarat en banque, and chemin de fer, are all descendants of this original Italian game of baccara, meaning zero and referring to the value of all 10-count cards. They soon became the exclusive games of the French nobility, not making their way to the public casinos for many years.

In European baccarat, in addition to the player's standing or drawing on 5 as he pleases, the play of the dealer, who operates the permanent bank for the casino, is completely optional. In spite of these options, the decisions of the banker in almost all cases is exactly the same as required by the rules of play for American baccarat. Perfect employment of these options would not increase the fixed percentage in favor of the casino by .5%. In this game, players who choose to bet with the bank to win are charged 5% of their winnings on each bet.

The game of baccarat en banque is very similar, with the exception that one bank hand and two player hands are dealt. Frequently the casino leases the bank as a concession to a syndicate who shares 50% of their monthly winnings with the casino, but in the event of a loss, the syndicate absorbs it all. In this version of the game, the player can bet on either or both of the player hands but never on the bank hand. The banker, a casino employee, can stand or draw as he chooses. Normally he will play according to the fixed American baccarat rules, but he can modify this procedure to enhance his chances of beating the player hand with the greatest amount of money bet on it.

The basic difference in the game of chemin de fer (which is French for railroad, and refers to the shoe moving around the table like a train) is that the bank rotates among the players and the house acts as a broker, collecting a fee from the winnings of each banker, therefore assuming no risk whatsoever. The player who is acting as banker cannot draw down any part of his original bank or subsequent winnings unless either the players do not subscribe to all the bank or, after the completion of any hand, the banker chooses to pass the bank. In this game, the player also has the choice of standing or drawing on 5, and the banker's play is completely optional. In any of these three games, the experienced American player who observed the European game long enough to become familiar with the variations in procedure would be able to play a professional game just by using the American baccarat rules.

TODAY'S GAME

Both European baccarat and chemin de fer have been offered in the United States from time to time, but the game played today combines the best features of each. All players can bet on either the banker or player hand, and although the shoe rotates among the players, who take turns playing the banker hand, all wagers are covered by the casino, and the bank, subject only to a maximum-bet size, is relatively unlimited. This version of the game, originating in South America and played in England and other parts of the world under the name of punto banco, was introduced into the United States in the late 1950's by Tommy Renzoni after the Castro government closed all the casinos in Cuba.

PLAYERS

Aimed primarily at high rollers, baccarat is a glamorous game with an old-world air of graciousness, and the patrons are usually the well-dressed, wealthy, older gamblers. The game is played with special chips and higher stakes in a small, luxuriously appointed, roped-off area and is dealt by tuxedoed croupiers in an atmosphere that is subdued and exclusive. Lady Luck is the predominant factor; whether you win or lose a bundle often depends on the turn of a single card, and the play is dictated by chance, not by choice.

In most casinos, minimum bets are either $5 or $20, although at certain times the minimum can be as high as $100. Maximum bets range from $1,000 to $2,000, but as usual, the larger casinos frequently raise the limit for well-heeled high rollers. Due to the common $20 minimum bet, baccarat tables furnish yellow $20 chips, which can be found nowhere else in the casino. $500 chips are available for larger wagers. Because of the relatively high level of betting, baccarat is not a very popular game, and most casinos offer just a few tables.

If you are not concerned about the elevated level of betting, don't be frightened by the fast pace of the game—about two hands a minute. Baccarat is the easiest of all the casino table games to learn, and no skill is required. Actually, you don't need to know the rules to play, even if you are given the shoe to deal. The croupiers will show you where to bet; when, where, and how to deal; and they will announce the winning hand. Everything is automatic.

As the cards are dealt, neither the banker, nor the croupiers, nor the players have any choice about standing or drawing cards. The fixed rules of the game always dictate the play. There are no options, and no decisions to make other than the size of your wager and whether you choose to bet on the banker or the player hand. The game could not be made any simpler.

CASINO CREW

Standing at the center of the layout are two croupiers, each responsible for selling chips and collecting the losing and paying off the winning wagers of their half of the table. Printed on the layout, directly in front of them, are fourteen small boxes numbered to correspond with the player betting spots, and used to keep track of any commissions owed by the players.

Opposite these dealers sits another croupier, the caller, who directs the game, telling the player with the shoe when to deal and to whom, and subsequently announcing the winning hand. The caller also removes the first card in the shoe after the shuffle and turns it faceup. The point value of this card, with face cards counting as ten for this purpose, determines how many cards are to be burned, and the caller then places them in the discard slot in the table, just in front of him. Cards from completed hands are also collected by the caller and deposited in this slot. This continues until the cut card appears in front of the shoe, signaling a new shuffle after the completion of that hand.

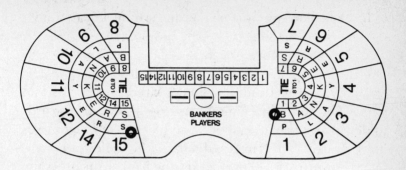

TABLE AND LAYOUT

Kidney-shaped to allow room for the dealers to reach out and handle both the bets and the cards, the table itself is about twelve feet long and three to four feet wide. The green baize covering is stenciled with a baccarat layout providing numbered boxes in front of each chair for players to wager on either the banker or player hand. The places are numbered from one to fifteen, with thirteen omitted, as few gamblers would be willing to sit and play at that traditionally unlucky spot.

The modern version of the ancient game of baccarat is played with eight decks, shuffled by the caller, cut by a player, and placed in a dealing box called a shoe, after the insertion of a cut card near the end of the combined decks to indicate the last hand. The shoe is then passed to a player at seat number one, who becomes the banker, although he may bet either hand. The shoe moves counterclockwise around the table each time the bank hand loses. Any player who becomes the banker may elect to pass the bank, then or at the completion of any hand, but to be eligible to deal, the banker must have at least a minimum bet on the table in either position.

After all wagers are placed, the banker alternately deals out four cards, facedown, first to the caller, who slides the cards to a player (traditionally the largest bettor for that hand), and second to himself, sliding these banker's cards under a corner of the shoe. The player then turns over his two cards and tosses them to the caller, who announces the total. Following this, the banker uncovers the two cards that were tucked under the corner of the shoe, and their value is called out by the croupier. The four suits have no meaning. At this point, a decision for the hand may have been reached with just these four cards. Tens and face cards count zero; all other cards count their point value; and if the hand totals more than 9, the left digit is disregarded; thus, unlike blackjack, no hand can bust. Totals of 8 or 9, called "naturals," are automatic winners, although of course a natural 9 beats a natural 8. If the player hand adds up to 6, 7, 8, or 9, or if the banker hand totals 7, 8, or 9, no additional cards are dealt and the hand that comes closest to a total of 9 wins and all bets are settled. Ties are a push; no money is exchanged and players are free to change their bets as they choose.

Frequently the totals of the two hands require a third card to be dealt to the player, the banker, or both. Neither one has a choice in the matter; the rules are fixed. Optimal strategy has been developed for every possible combination of cards, and since as many as fifteen players are wagering on just two hands, to avoid arguments over poor play, standing and drawing decisions are mandatory. Remember, though, neither player nor banker ever draws against a natural 8 or 9.

PLAYER RULES

HAVING	
1-2-3-4-5-10	DRAWS A CARD
6-7	STANDS
8-9	NATURAL Bank cannot draw.

BANK RULES

HAVING	DRAWS WHEN GIVING	DOES NOT DRAW WHEN GIVING
3	1-2-3-4-5-6-7-9-10	8
4	2-3-4-5-6-7	1-8-9-10
5	4-5-6-7	1-2-3-8-9-10
6	6-7	1-2-3-4-5-8-9-10
7	STANDS	
8-9	NATURAL Player cannot draw.	

RULES FOR PLAYER'S HAND

If the rules require the player to stand on his initial two cards, the caller announces, "Player stands with [point total]." But if the player must draw, the croupier calls,

"Card for the player." Only then does the banker deal a card faceup to the croupier, who places it next to the first two cards as he announces the new total. The decisions for the player hand are easy to learn. If the initial cards total 5 or less, draw one and only one card; otherwise stand. When the player hand is completed, the procedure for completing the banker hand is the same, but the rules for drawing or standing are a little more complicated.

RULES FOR BANKER'S HAND

Except for initial cards totaling 2 or less, which always require a draw, the decisions for the banker hand vary depending on the player's third card. Again, only one card may be drawn, and it's always taken if the banker's hand totals:

- 3 and the player stands or draws 1, 2, 3, 4, 5, 6, 7, 9, or 10.

- 4 and the player stands or draws 2, 3, 4, 5, 6, or 7.

- 5 and the player stands or draws 4, 5, 6, or 7.

- 6 and the player draws 6 or 7. The dealer must stand if the player stands.

Notice that the rules can require the banker to draw even when his first two cards beat the player's final hand, and a third card can cause the banker's hand to lose. When both hands are concluded, the caller declares the winner, announcing the point total for each.

Because the inherent odds of the game favor the banker over the player, the casinos assess a 5% commission on all winning bets on the banker so that the house advantage on either hand is about the same, 1.06% on the banker vs. 1.23% on the player. The casino pays even money on all bets, which amounts to an overpayment on winning banker bets, but you don't have to worry about keeping track of the commissions on these bets; the dealers do this for you with tokens that are placed in your numbered commission box in front of them, each time you bet and win on the banker's hand. The accumulated commissions are collected by the dealers while the cards are being shuffled for the next round, and they must be paid before you leave the table if you quit during a shoe. Always be aware of your commission indebtedness, and never bet your last chips before settling up.

Exhibit 7:
Casino Advantage at Baccarat

	%
Banker Hand	1.06
Player Hand	1.23
Tie	14.05

MATHEMATICS OF BACCARAT

The mathematics of baccarat are also relatively easy to understand. First, we must remember that $100 bet on the player hand will yield $100 when it wins, but the same bet on a winning banker hand yields only $95 because of the 5% commission. Now, let's consider the effect of the fixed drawing and standing rules. Using a formula from Allan N. Wilson's *The Casino Gambler's Guide,* we find that in the long run the hands will break down like this:

Banker hand wins   45.84% of all hands   50.68% disregarding
                                                          ties

Player hand wins   44.61% of all hands   49.32% disregarding
                                                          ties

Neither hand wins
(a tie)   9.55% of all hands_____
                          100. %   100. %

44.61% of the time,
$100 bet on the banker hand will lose $100 or $44.61

45.84% of the time,
$100 bet on the banker hand will win $95 or $43.55

9.55% of the time,
$100 bet on the banker hand will tie.   _____

Casino advantage, banker hand: 1.06

45.84% of the time,
$100 bet on the player hand will lose $100 or $45.84

44.61% of the time,
$100 bet on the player hand will win $100 or $44.61

9.55% of the time,
$100 bet on the player hand will tie   _____

Casino advantage, player hand: 1.23

There is only one other bet available on the baccarat layout, a wager that both hands will tie, paying 8 to 1.

Knowing that this will occur 9.55% of the time, let's see
how good a proposition this is:

90.45% of the time,
$100 bet on a tie will lose $100 or $90.45

9.55 of the time,
$100 bet on a tie will win $800 or $76.40

Casino advantage, tie-hand bet: 14.05

From this we can see that if we would like to lose our
money ten times as fast in baccarat, the best way to accomplish our goal would be to continually wager on a tie.

At one time, Las Vegas baccarat layouts provided for
betting on a natural 8 or 9, paying 9 to 1, and yielding
the casino about 5%. However, Edward O. Thorp, who
published the first card-counting system for blackjack, developed a baccarat card-counting strategy, enabling a
player to determine when the chance of a natural's being
dealt from the remaining decks increased. Based on the
fact that a surplus of 8's, 9's, and 10-count cards would
produce more naturals, the system was described in *Life*
magazine in 1964, and shortly after, all casinos eliminated
this option. Since then, no one has been able to devise a
card-counting strategy that would significantly alter the
house edge in baccarat.

If you would like to play a relaxed yet exciting, sophisticated casino game without bothering to learn complicated rules or strategies, baccarat may be the game for
you. There are really only two places to bet; the croupiers dictate the play of the cards, and your only major

decision is how much to wager. Unless you are foolish enough to bet on a tie, there are no mistakes that can be made: more than any other casino table game, baccarat depends simply on pure luck. Just remember the words of John Milton Hay, Teddy Roosevelt's Secretary of State: "True luck consists not in holding the best cards at the table. Luckiest is he who knows just when to rise and go home."

THE STREAK

Mr. K. is a high roller. There is no doubt about it. I got to know him when he called me about participating in my Blackjack Clinic. He told me that he had dropped $25,000 playing baccarat and he wanted to find a way to win it back. I told him that I could teach him how to win at blackjack, but that I couldn't guarantee how much he'd win.

Mr. K. took the Blackjack Clinic and became an excellent card counter and a disciplined blackjack player. Or so I thought. It turns out that he did win back his $25,000, although it wasn't just because of the 1.5% long-run advantage that I taught him how to achieve at blackjack. He had a series of very lucky sessions where all the cards were going his way. I told Mr. K. not to count on the same heavy winnings in every session and, sure enough, his luck turned; he dropped about $10,000. At that point he regressed to baccarat. He got lucky again and won back his $10,000 and then began alternating his play between blackjack and baccarat. Although he still plays an excellent game of blackjack, Mr. K. is a gambler—he possesses the gambler's urgency to play for high stakes. He seeks, as all true gamblers do, an "adrenaline high."

Recently Mr. K. invited me down to observe his play at the baccarat tables. Agreeing to meet in front of the baccarat pit prior to starting play, I arrived at the appointed time, only to find Mr. K. already in the game, looking very distressed. He had arrived two days earlier and was down about $10,000. Mr. K. expressed the usual gambler's lament about not quitting when he was ahead; at one point he had been up $5,000.

I sat down to play alongside Mr. K. Down to his last $500, he had used up his $4,000 credit line, so there was nothing he could do if he dropped that last $500. I watched it dwindle down to $50 and then talked him into having lunch.

During lunch I attempted to talk Mr. K. into going home, licking his wounds, and returning another day to play blackjack, where he could enjoy a 1.5% positive advantage instead of the negative one-plus percent at baccarat, but to no avail. In fact, he talked me into cashing a check for him for $1,000. I agreed on the condition that we would play blackjack. O.K. But we couldn't find a seat! Not even at a $25 table.

Mr. K. suggested baccarat. I reluctantly acquiesced. One table was full and one table was empty. Mr. K. chose the empty table with the exclamation, "Let it [the recoup or the wipeout] happen fast!"

Now, Mr. K. is a streak bettor, looking for a long series of wins in a row on either the bank or the players. He bets whatever has come up last until it loses: For example, if the bank wins, he keeps betting the bank until the players win. Then he jumps to the players until the bank wins, etc.

Well, it was Mr. K's lucky day, because we caught a shoe with a lot of streaks, starting with 16 straight wins for the players. Mr. K's betting progressed from $40 to $500. As I was willing to risk only $100, my betting progressed from $20 to $200 in a conservative progression as follows: 20-20-40-40-60-60-80-100-120-140-160-180-200.

This is one of the most amazing streaks I have ever seen in my twenty-two years of playing casino games. The odds of getting a group of sixteen wins in a row are about 65,000 to one. During the streak, there were certain things prescribed by Mr. K. to keep it going: the player's cards were turned over by the same person each time; the banker's cards were always tapped against Mr. K.'s chips; the only conversation allowed was in conjunction with the bet size; and counting chips won was prohibited. But this streak was not the last good thing to come out of this fantastic shoe; three or four other streaks of five or six wins occurred, and at the end of the shoe, Mr. K. had recouped his $10,000 and had won another $1,000 to boot. I had multiplied my $100 by sixteen. Our play had begun at 3:00 P.M., and at 4:03 P.M. we were cashing in at the cashier's cage.

There is no moral to this story, but I will give you some advice on baccarat. If you're feeling lucky, set aside part of your casino bankroll for a fling at the baccarat tables—maybe you'll catch a streak.

8.

Blackjack

HISTORY

Gambling with playing cards spread steadily throughout Europe after Johann Gutenberg printed the first deck in Germany in 1440, and many of the games involved drawing cards to reach a certain total. Although the exact relationship remains obscure, blackjack is believed to have evolved from several of these early games. Baccarat, with the magic number of 9, appeared in Italy about 1490, followed by the game of seven and a half, which seems to be the first game where the player automatically lost if he went over the desired number. The game of one and thirty was first played sometime before 1570 in Spain, and the Duke of Wellington, the Marquess of Queensbury, and Prime Minister Disraeli all played quinze (15) in Crockford's, the famous English casino which flourished between 1827 and 1844. From France came *trente et quarante* (30 and 40) and finally *vingt un* or *vingt et un* (21 or 20 and 1), which crossed the Atlantic ocean and was listed in the *American Hoyle* of 1875.

As first played in the United States, it was a private game, but by 1910, tables for twenty-one were being offered in the gambling parlors of Evansville, Indiana. Acceptance was slow, and to stimulate interest, in 1912 operators offered to pay 3 to 2 for any count of 21 in the first two cards, and 10 to 1 if the 21 consisted of the ace of spades and either the jack of spades or the jack of clubs. This hand was called, of course, blackjack. The 10-to-1 payoff was soon eliminated, but the term remained, first as the name of any two-card 21 hand, and subsequently as the name of the game itself, although twenty-one would have been more appropriate.

By 1919, tables covered with green baize and emblazoned in gold letters announcing "Blackjack Pays Odds of 3 to 2" were being manufactured in Chicago and appeared in gambling halls throughout the country. The popularity of the game grew slowly until gambling was legalized in Nevada in 1931, and blackjack soon became the third-most-successful game, outstripping faro, but trailing both roulette and craps. Because of the prohibitive casino edge of 5.26% in roulette, discouraged players drifted away from the game, and by 1948 blackjack had become the second-biggest casino moneymaker.

TODAY'S GAME

This continued until 1956, when a book was published by Baldwin, Cantey, Maisel, and McDermott containing a nearly perfect basic strategy, followed in 1962 by Edward

O. Thorp's book, which refined the strategy and added a counting system. Now, for the first time, the sophisticated gambler could learn to play nearly even with the house, and perhaps with a slight edge in his favor. This scientifically developed information sparked a nationwide interest in blackjack that has made it the number-one game in American casinos today.

Because the table is less than half the size of those required for craps, roulette, or baccarat, with a corresponding reduction in both the number of players and casino personnel, blackjack is far less intimidating to the beginning player. Couple this with the simplicity of the basic rules—both the player and the dealer draw cards and whoever comes closest to 21 without going over wins—and we can understand the constantly expanding popularity of the game.

Blackjack is unique among all the casino games inasmuch as any player can make decisions that will affect the results of the game. In addition, it is the only game where the outcome of one hand influences the following hands. Since the type of cards that have been played determines the value of the cards remaining to be played, the probability of winning or losing is in a constant state of flux, and although chance is still a significant factor, the skillful player enjoys a marked advantage over the novice. Obviously, the casinos are a profit-making institution, so why do they continue to offer a game where the player has a fair chance? Elementary, my dear reader: Over ninety percent of all players do not make a sufficient effort to learn the fundamentals of the game. Ironically, the fact that the game can be beaten is well known to the casino operators, but since very few players can be bothered to invest the necessary time to learn to play, blackjack has become the most profitable table game in the house.

PLAYERS

New casinos are still being designed and built, both in Nevada and Atlantic City, and thousands of new casino gamers are trying their luck every day. Many of these neophytes know little or nothing about how to play or how to bet. To accommodate these newcomers, as well as the multitude of existing players who are not playing to their best advantage, let's thoroughly explore the basic elements of the game.

First of all, although you will find seven betting spots on the table, blackjack is not a group game. Each bettor is playing against the dealer and betting against the house; the number of players or where they sit has no effect on the ultimate outcome. Second, as far as the average player is concerned, the game is played with a continuous deck. The flow of cards is random, and the decision to draw or not draw by any one player has no long-run effect on other players. Of course, in any one hand, the player to the right of you or the dealer appears to have significant control of the results of your hand, but really, the draw of each player at the table has an equal effect on the hand. Nevertheless, many players critically observe the play of the hand preceding the dealer, commonly called "third base," with the result that most beginners shun this chair to avoid contention. Ninety percent of the bettors are there to enjoy themselves, and because of the game's frequent pauses for shuffling, dealing, and settling bets, you'll find an air of relaxation that is rare at the other games. So if you happen to sit where there are disagreeable players, move to another table. They are almost always plentiful.

As soon as you sit down, you'll need chips. Place some currency alongside the betting circle directly in front of you; the dealer will announce the amount to the pit supervisor and exchange it for distinctly decorated plastic disks, setting them in front of you as he pushes your money through the slot in the table into the concealed drop box. All the tables carry $1, $5, and $25 chips, frequently colored white, red, and green in Atlantic City, and some tables keep $100 chips, usually black. The dealer's rack also contains pink $2.50 chips and half-dollars, but these are used only for settling odd bets such as the 3-to-2 payoff for a blackjack on a $3 or $5 wager. If you want to change a large-denomination chip for smaller ones, place it alongside your betting spot and announce, "Change, please." Never place it in the circle, as it may be mistaken for a bet.

Although state regulations in New Jersey prohibit the betting of cash, money wagers may be made in Nevada. However, most casinos prefer the use of chips. Skillful dealers can add up the value of a stack of mixed chips in an instant because of the various colors; however all currency is green and the bills must be checked and rechecked. Casinos also realize that many bettors subconsciously do not place the same value on chips that they do on actual cash. Somehow many people feel that once they give up their money for chips, it's not really theirs anymore; subsequently players find it infinitely easier to push out four green chips than to reach in their wallet and extract a $100 bill.

New Jersey regulations also prohibit the using of chips from one casino in another, but this practice used to be prevalent in Nevada. However, because junketeers, who were required to buy in for a certain sum in order to qualify for complimentary rooms, meals, and travel, frequently reneged on their obligation to play at the tables by converting their chips to cash in other casinos, the interchange of chips between casinos has just about become a thing of the past.

As you stack your chips, you may notice one or two small signs displayed near the dealer. One often lists the casino's particular blackjack rules, and the other indicates the minimum and maximum bets in effect at that particular table. Minimum-bet sizes may be $2, $3, $5, $10, $15, $25, $50, and $100; but $2 and $3 minimums are often hard to find, and the most common table size seems to be $5 or $25. Although maximum bets usually range up to $1,000, pit bosses have special signs available for high rollers, and $2,000 or $3,000 maximums are not unusual. Occasionally, the entire table will be roped off for a really big bettor.

All bets must be placed before any cards are dealt, and many casinos will permit you to place additional wagers in adjacent vacant positions. Procedures for betting more than one hand vary from casino to casino, so check with the dealer if this type of betting appeals to you. Incidentally, when you have finished playing, the dealer can't reconvert your chips into money, but he will be more than willing to change them for larger denominations. For cash, you must take your chips to the cashier's cage.

CASINO CREW

While the players are making their bets, the dealer will be thoroughly shuffling from one to six decks of cards. Upon finishing, in a single-deck game, the dealer places the pack in front of any player, who is expected to lift off the top half and place it on the table next to the bottom half. In a multi-deck game, the player is given a colored cut card which is to be inserted anywhere in the stack of cards placed on the table but held by the dealer. Some people prefer not to cut, and the option is then given to the next player. If no one wants to cut, the dealer does it himself. After the cut is completed, the dealer places the colored card toward the back of the stack to indicate when to reshuffle. If it's a single-deck game, the dealer will hold the cards, but in a multideck game the cards are placed in a wooden or plastic dealing box called a shoe. In any case, the first card—called a burn card—is not used, but is placed on the bottom of the single deck or in a discard rack. This card is not usually shown, but in many cases the dealer will expose it when a player asks.

Starting with the player on his left, often called "first base," and continuing in a clockwise direction, the dealer gives each player a card and himself one faceup; then he deals each player a second card, and this time his card is placed, facedown, under the dealer up-card. Both of the players' cards are usually dealt facedown in the single-deck game and faceup in multideck play, but whether the cards are exposed or not, the game is played in the same manner. Although many bettors prefer the single deck with its feeling of secrecy as they peek at their cards, the trend is overwhelmingly toward the multideck game. Not only is faceup play much faster, and therefore more profitable for the casino, but since bettors are not permitted to touch their cards, the opportunity for player cheating is nearly eliminated.

When everyone has his initial two cards, again starting at first base, each bettor is permitted to draw additional cards, which are always dealt one at a time, faceup. If the player goes over 21, he loses; his bet is collected, and his cards are placed with the rest of the discards. After each player has acted on his hand, the dealer must then complete his own hand, based on fixed rules printed on the table covering. The dealer's play is not affected by the players' exposed hands; his decisions are mechanical. If the dealer does not go over 21, called breaking, he collects from players with hands totaling less than his, pays off players with hands better than his, and ties, or pushes, with players holding hands of equal value.

Now you are ready for the next hand, which is dealt from the remaining cards. This continues until the colored cut card appears, signaling a reshuffle after the completion of the hand in progress, and the entire procedure is repeated. As you play, you may notice a well-dressed person with an air of authority casually observing the dealer, the players, and the action; this is the pit boss, who is responsible for a group of tables and settles all disputes. His decisions are final.

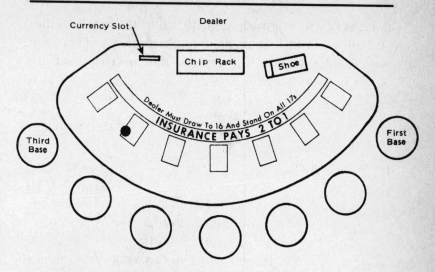

TABLE AND LAYOUT

About three feet by five feet, semicircular in shape, and covered with green felt, the table is usually imprinted with the payoff for blackjack, the dealer's drawing and standing rules, a curved betting line for insurance wagers, betting positions for six or seven players, and the casino logo. Chairs for players are provided around the perimeter, facing the dealer, who stands behind the chip rack, usually with a dealing shoe on his left and a discard tray on his right.

Before the game is started, the dealer spreads the cards to be used across the table, first facedown so the backs can be inspected for telltale markings, and then faceup, enabling both the dealer and the players to ascertain that there are no extra or missing cards. Standard 52-card poker-sized decks are used, and the four suits have no significance; only the numerical value of each card is important: 2's through 9's are counted at their point value, and all 10's and face cards are valued at ten. The ace is unique, and can be counted as one or eleven at the player's option.

BLACKJACK

After receiving the initial two cards, you determine their value by simply adding them together. A 5 and 3 is eight; a king and 6 is sixteen; and an ace and 7 is either eight or eighteen. If your first two cards consist of an ace and a 10 or any picture card, the hand is a perfect one—a "blackjack"—often called a natural. Unless the dealer ties you with another blackjack, you have an automatic winner, and instead of the usual even-money payoff, you are immediately paid one and a half times your bet—if you have $10 up, you receive $15. With a tie, called a push, no money is exchanged.

HARD AND SOFT HANDS

All hands not containing an ace are known as hard hands, and any hand including an ace that can be valued as eleven is called a soft hand. For example, an A-5 is a soft sixteen; if hit with a 2, the hand becomes a soft eighteen; if another card is drawn, for instance a 9, the ace is revalued as one and the final hand now becomes a hard seventeen. Any hard hand of twelve through sixteen is known as a stiff, or breaking hand.

OBJECTIVE

Let's now consider the objective of casino blackjack. Many blackjack books define the objective as getting a hand as close as possible to 21. This is not always true. Your objective is to beat the dealer, and learning this lesson is your first step on the road to becoming a winning blackjack player. It is possible to beat the dealer by holding a hand that is far less than 21—a twelve or thirteen for example. Remember there are two ways to win, by holding a higher hand than the dealer, and by not hitting a breaking hand and waiting for the dealer to break. This is a decision that many beginning players seldom make. Thinking they must always get as close as possible to 21, they hit more often than they should, thus breaking more often and contributing to the casino edge of up to 6% over the nonsystem player.

Casino rules are defined to give the dealer one major advantage and one major disadvantage. His advantage is he always draws last. If he breaks after you have broken—in reality a tie—he has already collected your chips, and he does not return them. The dealer's disadvantage is that he must draw to sixteen or less; therefore, with hands totaling twelve to sixteen, it's possible that the next card may break him. You, the player, can capitalize on this handicap by making judicious decisions about drawing or standing.

Many players lose because they hit too often; other novices, unrealistically hoping for the dealer to break, do not hit enough. These hitting and standing decisions cannot be made by hunch; logic must be used. If the dealer's up-card is 2, 3, 4, or 5, you know he must hit, no matter what the value of his hole card is; therefore, you would stand on a lower hand value, such as thirteen, and hope for the dealer to break. On the other hand, if the dealer has a high up-card, for instance a 9 or 10, you would hit and try to get as close to 21 as possible because there is a good chance that the dealer's hole card is also high, and with a hand greater than sixteen he wouldn't have to draw. After making your hitting and standing decisions, if you haven't broken, you wait for the dealer to deal to the other players and then to himself. Then your bet is paid off at even money if you win, collected if you lose, or left alone if you tie.

OPTIONS

The characteristic that makes blackjack unique among all casino games is the many player options. After you receive your first two cards, in addition to the option of hitting and standing, under certain conditions you are allowed to split your hand, double your bet, insure your hand, or if you are not satisfied with your cards, sometimes you can surrender them and get half your money back. Almost all decisions are indicated to the dealer by the way you move your hand or where you place additional chips after your original wager is made. Let's look at these decisions and their signals; just remember in Atlantic City and many other places where multidecks are used, you are never permitted to touch your cards or your initial bet.

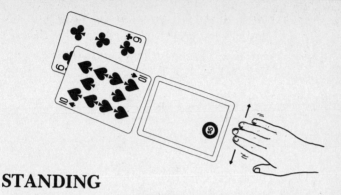

STANDING

The player always has the option of standing, even with the first two cards. In Atlantic City casinos as well as in many others, you must give a hand rather than a verbal signal. To indicate to the dealer you wish to stand, simply wave your hand, palm down, over your cards. The dealer will then move to the next player.

HITTING

If you are not satisfied with the total of your hand, you may draw one or more cards as long as you don't break, or go over 21. To call for a hit, either point at your cards or make a beckoning motion with your fingers. When the hit card breaks your hand, the dealer will automatically scoop up your bet and place your cards in the discard tray, as you have lost, even if the dealer subsequently breaks.

SPLITTING PAIRS

When the first two cards you receive are of equal value, you may elect to split them and play each as a separate hand, drawing until you are satisfied or break—first to the card on your right, and second to the card on your left. Two ten-value cards, such as a king and a jack, can also be split, but when aces are split, most casinos permit only one card to be drawn to each. If a ten-value card is drawn to a split ace, or vice versa, the resulting hand is considered a 21, not a blackjack, and is paid off at 1 to 1. This 21 would tie any dealer 21 but would lose to a dealer blackjack. In many casinos if a pair is split and a third card of the same rank is drawn, the hand may be resplit. However, this is not permitted in Atlantic City. To indicate to the dealer your desire to split, merely slide up another bet of equal value next to your first wager, touching neither your cards nor the original bet. In some casinos, including those in Atlantic City, you may double down after you split. This procedure is explained next.

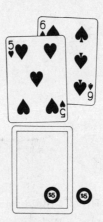

DOUBLING DOWN

When you think that with just one more card in addition to your first two you will beat the dealer, you are allowed to double your original bet and draw one—and only one—card. While many casinos will permit you to double down on any initial hand except two cards totaling 21, some restrict this option to totals of 10 and 11. To signal the dealer your intention to double, place another bet, up to the amount of your original wager, alongside your first bet. Since you will always have the advantage when you take this option, you should double for the full amount. Again, to minimize the chances for player cheating, you are not permitted to touch either your cards or your original bet. When you split a pair, many casinos will permit you to double after you draw the first card to each of the split hands. A few casinos will allow you to double

down on a hand of 10 or 11 consisting of more than two
cards.

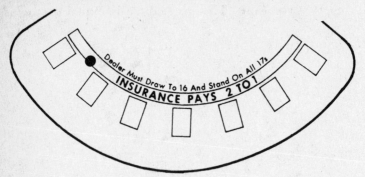

INSURANCE

Whenever the dealer's up-card is an ace, before proceeding with the hand, he will ask, "Insurance, anyone?"
If you believe the dealer's hole card is a 10 for blackjack,
you are permitted to place a side bet up to half of your
original wager on the Insurance line in front of you. If,
indeed, the dealer does have a 10, you are immediately
paid 2 to 1 on your insurance bet, but lose your original
wager unless you too have blackjack and tie the dealer.
You are not really insuring anything; you are simply betting that the dealer's unseen card is a 10. Since the insurance payoff is 2 to 1, never make an insurance bet unless
you are counting cards and know that the ratio of
non-10's to 10's in the undealt cards is less than 2 to 1.
This "no-insurance" rule applies even when the player
has a blackjack. Many people, including otherwise knowledgeable players, will urge you to insure a blackjack
against a dealer's ace, assuring you that you can't lose.

They are correct; you will win something; however, in the long run you will win less.

SURRENDER

A few casinos offer the option of surrender. If you are not satisfied with your chances of beating the dealer after seeing your first two cards, you may announce, "Surrender"; the dealer will pick up your cards and collect half your bet, returning the other half to you. This is the only decision in blackjack that is indicated verbally. Where the dealer is required to first check his hole card for blackjack, the option is called "late surrender." If you are permitted to turn in your hand before the dealer checks for blackjack (no longer allowed in Atlantic City), the decision is termed "early surrender."

DEALER'S PLAY

After offering cards to all players, the dealer exposes his hole card. If there are players who still have cards, the dealer then acts on his hand according to fixed rules, with none of the player options. When the dealer's cards total 17 or more, he must stand, and with a hand of 16 or less, the dealer must hit until he reaches 17 or better. If the dealer breaks, all remaining players win. In most casinos, the dealer must count an ace in his hand as 11 if it will raise his hand to 17, 18, 19, 20, or 21. A few casinos make an exception to this rule and require the dealer to hit

A-6, or soft 17. It is important to note that the dealer has no choice in the matter. If all the players have hands totaling 18, 19, 20, or 21, the dealer must still stand with a 17—an obvious loser. Likewise, if the players show hands totaling 12, 13, 14, or 15, the dealer must still hit his 16 and risk breaking an otherwise winning hand. If the dealer does not break, and reaches a hand between 17 and 21, proceeding counterclockwise from third base, he collects from players with lower hands, pays off at even money the players with higher hands, and pushes or ties those with equal hands, indicating this with a tap of the back of his fingers in front of the player's cards. Players are now free to pick up winnings, if any, and make a new bet as the whole process is repeated.

BASIC STRATEGY

Most occasional gamblers are unaware of the tremendous amount of research that has been done to provide blackjack players with winning strategies. This research has been performed with the aid of high-speed computers by some of the best mathematical minds in the country. The original basic strategy, a simple set of decision rules dependent on the player's first two cards and the dealer's up-card, was published in 1956 by four Army officers—Roger R. Baldwin, Wilbert E. Cantey, Herbert Maisel, and James McDermott—after three years of painstaking work with desk calculators. Subsequently, the result of their work was confirmed and further refined by Dr. Edward O. Thorp and Julian M. Braun, who simulated the play of millions of hands on an IBM computer and provided a basic strategy that has made blackjack, properly played, a near-even game.

This strategy, designed to win more of your good hands and lose fewer of your bad hands, yields the best, or most profitable, decisions applying to all the blackjack options—standing, hitting, splitting, doubling, and surrendering. To understand the strategy, though, you must remember the three variables involved in making blackjack decisions—your two cards and the dealer's up-card. There are 550 possible combinations of these two hands; therefore, there are 550 different blackjack decisions. Fortunately, many of these decisions are similar, and about 30 rules cover all of them. I cannot say too often that playing basic strategy is a must for both the casual and serious blackjack player, so thoroughly learn the strategy for the game you expect to play most frequently. You will notice that the following strategies covering single and multideck games vary very little, and occasionally using the rules for your basic game in another game will have only a very small effect on your expectations.

Exhibit 8:
Basic Strategy for Atlantic City Shoe Game

Player's Hand	Rules for Dealer's Up-Cards
5	Always hit
6	Always hit
7	Always hit

Player's Hand	Rules for Dealer's Up-Cards
8	Always hit
9	Double on 3–6, otherwise hit
10	Double on 2–9, hit on 10–A
11	Double on 2–10, hit on A
12	Stand on 4–6, otherwise hit
13	Stand on 2–6, otherwise hit
14	Stand on 2–6, otherwise hit
15	Stand on 2–6, otherwise hit
16	Stand on 2–6, otherwise hit
17–21	Always stand
A,2	Double on 5–6, otherwise hit
A,3	Double on 5–6, otherwise hit
A,4	Double on 4–6, otherwise hit
A,5	Double on 4–6, otherwise hit
A,6	Double on 3–6, otherwise hit
A,7	Double on 3–6, stand on 2, 7, 8, hit on 9, 10, A
A,8	Always stand
A,9–A,10	Always stand
A,A	Always split
2,2	Split on 2–7, otherwise hit
3,3	Split on 2–7, otherwise hit
4,4	Split on 5–6, otherwise hit
5,5	Double on 2–9, hit on 10–A

Player's Hand	Rules for Dealer's Up-Cards
6,6	Split on 2–6, otherwise hit
7,7	Split on 2–7, otherwise hit
8,8	Always split
9,9	Split on 2–6, 8, 9, stand on 7, 10, A
10,10	Always stand

Exhibit 9:
Basic Strategy for Las Vegas Single Deck

Player's Hand	Rules for Dealer's Up-Cards
5	Always hit
6	Always hit
7	Always hit
8	Double on 5–6, otherwise hit (if 6,2 always hit)
9	Double on 2–6, otherwise hit
10	Double on 2–9, hit on 10–A
11	Always double
12	Stand on 4–6, otherwise hit (if 10,2 stand on 5, otherwise hit)
13	Stand on 2–6, otherwise hit
14	Stand on 2–6, otherwise hit
15	Stand on 2–6, otherwise hit

Player's Hand	Rules for Dealer's Up-Cards
16	Stand on 2–6, otherwise hit
17–21	Always stand
A,2	Double on 4–6, otherwise hit
A,3	Double on 4–6, otherwise hit
A,4	Double on 4–6, otherwise hit
A,5	Double on 4–6, otherwise hit
A,6	Double on 2–6, otherwise hit
A,7	Double on 3–6, stand on 2,7,8,A, hit on 9,10
A,8	Double on 6, otherwise stand
A,9–A,10	Always stand
A,A	Always split
2,2	Split on 3–7, otherwise hit
3,3	Split on 4–7, otherwise hit
4,4	Double on 5–6, otherwise hit
5,5	Double on 2–9, hit on 10-A
6,6	Split on 2–6, otherwise hit
7,7	Split on 2–7, stand on 10, otherwise hit
8,8	Always split
9,9	Split on 2–6, 8,9, stand on 7,10,A
10,10	Always stand

If the casino allows doubling down after splitting pairs (e.g., the El Cortez), you would add the following pair-split rules to those above:

Split 2,2 on dealer 2

Split 3,3 on dealer 2,3 or 8

Split 4,4 on dealer 4,5 or 6

Split 6,6 on dealer 7

Split 7,7 on dealer 8

If the casino allows surrendering, you would modify the above rules and surrender the following hands:

1. Against a dealer ace you would surrender:

10,6

2. Against a dealer 10 or face card you would surrender:

7,7; 9,6; 9,7; 10,5; 10,6

Exhibit 10:
Basic Strategy for Reno-Tahoe Single Deck

Player's Hand	Rules for Dealer's Up-Cards
5	Always hit
6	Always hit
7	Always hit
8	Always hit
9	Always hit
10	Double on 2–9, hit on 10–A
11	Always double
12	Stand on 4–6, otherwise hit
13	Stand on 2–6, otherwise hit
14	Stand on 2–6, otherwise hit
15	Stand on 2–6, otherwise hit

Player's Hand	Rules for Dealer's Up-Cards
16	Stand on 2–6, otherwise hit
17–21	Always stand
A,2	Always hit
A,3	Always hit
A,4	Always hit
A,5	Always hit
A,6	Always hit
A,7	Stand on 2–8, otherwise hit
A,8	Always stand
A,9–A,10	Always stand
A,A	Always split
2,2	Split on 3–7, otherwise hit
3,3	Split on 4–7, otherwise hit
4,4	Always hit
5,5	Double on 2–9, hit on 10–A
6,6	Split on 2–6, otherwise hit
7,7	Split on 2–7, stand on 10, otherwise hit
8,8	Always split
9,9	Split on 2–6, 8,9, stand on 7,10,A
10,10	Always stand

Exhibit 11:
Basic Strategy for Nevada Shoe Game

The following matrix can be used to tailor a basic strategy to any Nevada shoe, single deck, or double deck game with the noted rules varations.

Your Hand	Rules for Dealer's Up-Cards									
	2	3	4	5	6	7	8	9	10	A
5,3	H	H	H	H [D]	H [D]	H	H	H	H	H
6,2	H	H	H	H	H	H	H	H	H	H
9	H [D]	D	D	D	D	H	H	H	H	H
10	D	D	D	D	D	D	D	D	H	H
11	D	D	D	D	D	D	D	D	D	H [D]
10,2	H	H	S [H]	S	S [H]	H	H	H	H	H
Other										
12s	H	H	S	S	S	H	H	H	H	H
13	S	S	S	S	S	H	H	H	H	H

Rules for Dealer's Up-Cards

Your Hand	2	3	4	5	6	7	8	9	10	A
14	S	S	S	S	S	H	H	H	H	H
15	S	S	S	S	S	H	H	H	H	H
16	S	S	S	S	S	H	H	H	H	H
17–21	S	S	S	S	S	S	S	S	S	S
A,2	H	H	H [D]	D	D	H	H	H	H	H
A,3	H	H	H [D]	D	D	H	H	H	H	H
A,4	H	H	D	D	D	H	H	H	H	H
A,5	H	H	D	D	D	H	H	H	H	H
A,6	H [D]	D	D	D	D	H	H	H	H	H
A,7	S	D	D	D	D	S	S	H	H	H [S]
A,8	S	S	S	S	S [D]	S	S	S	S	S
A,9	S	S	S	S	S	S	S	S	S	S
A,A	P	P	P	P	P	P	P	P	P	P
2,2	H (P)	[P] H (P)	P	P	P	P	H	H	H	H

3,3	H (P)	H (P)	H*	P	P	P	H*	H	H	H
4,4	H	H	H*	H (P) [D]	H (P) [D]	H	H	H	H	H
5,5	D	D	D	D	D	D	D	D	H	H
6,6	H (P) [P]	H (P)	P	P	P	P	H*	H	H	H
7,7	P	P	P	P	P	P	H*	H	H [S]	H
8,8	P	P	P	P	P	P	P	P	P	P
9,9	P	P	P	P	P	S	P	P	S	S
10,10	S	S	S	S	S	S	S	S	S	S

Code: [ ] One-deck variations

(P) Split if doubling down after splitting (P stands for pair split) allowed—takes precedence over doubling on 4,4 versus 5 and 6.

* Split if DDAS and one-deck (DDAS stands for double down after split).

NOTE: If you are playing a two-deck game, the preceding four-deck strategy should be used with two exceptions:

9—Double on 2–6; otherwise, hit.

11—If 9–2 or 8–3, hit on ace; otherwise, double.

If the casino allows surrendering, you would modify these rules and surrender the following hands in a four-deck game:

1. Against a dealer ace you would surrender:
9,7; 10,6
2. Against a dealer 10 or face card you would surrender:
9,6; 9,7; 10,5; 10,6
3. Against a dealer 9 you would surrender:
9,7; 10,6

CARD COUNTING

The theory of card counting is covered in great detail in my earlier books, *Blackjack: A Winner's Handbook* and *Blackjack's Winning Formula*. The following includes material excerpted from those books.

Blackjack and the computer make perfect marriage partners. The courtship began in the late fifties when four Army engineers, Baldwin, Cantey, Maisel, and McDermott, developed the first basic strategy—a set of rules for standing, hitting, splitting, and doubling down. The engagement occurred in the early sixties when Dr. Edward Thorp, using an IBM computer, proved that blackjack could be beaten by keeping track of the tens as they are played. Julian Braun, of the IBM Corporation, consummated this marriage by simulating the play of millions of blackjack hands on his high-speed computers to refine the basic strategy and Thorp's card-counting techniques.

The reason that computers and blackjack make such good bedfellows is that blackjack rules are well defined and can be easily programmed. Computers were needed to study the game because of the millions of calculations required to determine when to make each decision and for determining the impact of a shortage or surplus of tens on the player's odds. Three million hands were simulated, for example, to determine whether or not the player should split a pair of fours with a six showing as the dealer's up-card.

With all this attention on blackjack, the game flourished as Dr. Thorp's book, *Beat the Dealer*, became a bestseller. Thousands of would-be card counters poured into Las Vegas every weekend looking for some easy money. Handicapped by not understanding basic money-management techniques—how much to bet in proportion to their total bankroll—they usually went home broke. In addition, not many players had the powers of concentration and mental capacity required to use the complicated card-counting formula detailed in Thorp's book. Of course, there were some big winners; bankrolled by two well-heeled high rollers, Thorp himself won tens of thousands of dollars in Nevada and Caribbean casinos, but because of these highly publicized winnings, he was eventually barred from play in all Nevada casinos.

Julian Braun's computer studies produced a plethora

of data that led to the development of a number of advanced blackjack systems. By the early seventies, scores of these systems were on the market, but because of their complexity, relatively few players were able to exploit them enough to win any significant amount. A number of these big winners, now also barred from the casinos, turned to systems-selling as a way to make a fast buck, besieging the occasional gambler with promises of quick riches and a life of luxury and travel—just by playing winning blackjack in glamorous casinos all over the world. Inexpensive books were published as a come-on for the higher-priced systems that the authors were really touting, and extremely expensive paperbacks—many virtually worthless—were sold in high-pressure direct-mail campaigns. "Blackjack Millionaires" appeared on television shows to plug their products, while national publications, such as *The Wall Street Journal* and *Life,* printed lead articles on this extraordinary phenomenon—the game in which the casino could be beaten.

With all this publicity, blackjack soon overtook craps as the most popular casino game, and the systems-sellers made fat profits. As more would-be counters learned the game, the casinos added more tables to accommodate the influx of players. But then followed an interesting paradox—casino profits increased! Not only did their total profits increase, but their rate of profit increased. Proportionately, casino winnings were increasing faster than the number of players. Why? Because too many occasional players were being taken in by the false promises of the systems-sellers. It's extremely difficult to apply all the data embodied in the more complicated card-counting systems, and players, rushing into action too soon and with too small a bankroll to cover their inevitable losing cycles, didn't realize that the big winners had spent countless hours practicing and possessed the self-discipline necessary to become inured to the many distractions of the casino environment.

Playing perfect basic strategy will eliminate the casino advantage of up to 6% and allow you to play an essentially even game, but to gain up to a 1.5% edge over the casino, you must learn how to count cards. In blackjack, the probability of winning the next hand depends on the type of cards remaining to be played. By keeping track of the cards as they are dealt, you can determine the chances of winning; if the chances are better than even, you raise the bet, and if the chances are even or less, you make a minimum bet. Not all cards are counted, only those that most directly affect the probability of winning, and in most card-counting systems, these are the high and low cards. The odds are in favor of the player when the decks remaining to be played contain a surplus of tens and aces, because more blackjacks and more standing hands of 17, 18, 19, and 20 will be dealt. Of course the dealer will also receive an equal share of these better hands, but he does not get paid 3 to 2 for blackjack; he cannot double down on 9, 10, or 11 with an improved chance of drawing a ten; he cannot split a pair when the odds are in his favor, and he must always hit his stiff hands of 12, 13, 14, 15, and 16 with an increased chance of breaking.

To become a successful card counter and a winning blackjack player, you must develop three skills:

- Learn the basic strategy so well that you can apply it without thinking.

- Learn to count cards swiftly and accurately.

- Learn to bet properly and manage your money.

This last skill—money management—is really more important than the others. Many blackjack players learn to become excellent card counters, only to fail because overbetting causes them to go broke. It never ceases to amaze me that an excellent counter will spend innumerable hours developing his skill and then walk into a casino with a $500 bankroll and make $25 bets. Twenty losing hands and he is wiped out.

The card-counting system described below, called High-Low, is one of the best of the fifty-plus point-count systems available today—some selling for as much as $200. First developed by Harvey Dubner in 1963, and initially printed in the second edition of Dr. Thorp's *Beat the Dealer*, it has most recently been published in Stanford Wong's *Professional Blackjack* and *How to Play Winning Blackjack* by Julian Braun. Simple to learn and effective to use, High-Low is played as follows:

- 2, 3, 4, 5, 6—the low cards—count as +1

- 7, 8, 9—the neutral cards—count as 0

- 10, J, Q, K, A—the high cards—count as −1

Simply start at zero with a freshly shuffled shoe and count each card. For example, if the following cards are played: 2, 4, 5, 10, J, 7, 8, 6, 4, 5, 5—count as follows: +1 (the 2), +2 (the 4), +3 (the 5), +2 (the 10 counts as −1), +1 (the J), +1 (the 7 counts as zero), +1 (the 8), +2 (the 6), +3 (the 4), +4 (the 5), +5 (the 5). When the count is plus, the deck is favorable because more low cards have been played; more high cards remain to be played, and in this situation the player should definitely increase the bet. Conversely, if the count is minus, more 10's, face cards, and aces have been played and the advantage is in favor of the casino.

Although the High-Low system is easy to learn, it does take considerable practice before it can be applied in a casino. Here is one exercise to help you prepare for actual play. Take a single deck of cards; turning one card over at a time, start with zero and keep a running count. When you finish, the deck total should be zero because the twenty high cards balance out the twenty low cards and, of course, the twelve neutral cards have no effect. When you can consistently do this in less than thirty seconds, you are ready to tackle the casinos.

STRIKING IT RICH WITH A RICH DECK

It's the dinner hour at one of the larger Atlantic City casinos. Throngs of people are crowding the restaurants, leaving a number of vacant seats at the blackjack tables. A distinguished-looking man, conservatively dressed in suit and tie, enters and casually strolls around the $25 tables. Singling one out, he sits down and makes a $100 bet.

He is dealt a twenty, with the dealer showing a four.

After the other players complete their hands, the dealer turns over a nine, hits with another nine, and breaks. The gentleman is paid off and leaves the entire $200 in his betting circle. Now he is dealt an eleven; the dealer shows a ten. Cooly he bets a second $200 on the hand and draws one more card—a ten for a perfect twenty-one. The dealer turns over a ten for a total of twenty. Our player calmly picks up his chips and leaves the table, the pit, and the casino $500 richer. He doesn't even bother to cash in.

That was a card counter in action. While strolling he was carefully watching for beginning games, timing his arrival at the table so he could scan the exposed initial cards, searching for a favorable count. As soon as the count dropped, he left. Although he wins only about half of his hands, his pattern of playing only when the deck is positive together with bet variation gives him a considerable edge.

Now let's look at another card counter in another Atlantic City casino. Also picking a time when he can play at uncrowded tables, he follows a similar pattern. Chips flow back and forth across the table as the player's stack fluctuates between fifteen and twenty-five green ($25) chips. Making minimum bets, he's waiting for a hot deck—rich in tens and aces. He gets it. Raising his bet to $100, he draws a thirteen against a dealer two. He stands. The dealer flips over a ten and hits his hand with a breaking ten. Our player smiles. More hands are played and he is winning consistently, making all the right decisions, doubling down when he is supposed to, and splitting pairs when it is to his advantage. After only thirty minutes of play, he is $1,000 ahead. He stays.

Now the villain enters—the pit boss. His job is to keep an eye on six to eight games and make sure everything is going smoothly. If there is a dispute, he settles it. He also watches for counters. Spotting our player early in his session, he waits for the evidence to build up, noticing the precision play—splitting a pair of tens against a six for example, and pulling a ten to each hand. The verdict is in and the heat is on. Whispering instructions in the dealer's ear, the pit boss is watching the counter like a hawk. When our player increases his bet from $50 to $400 to take advantage of a very favorable count, the boss moves in for the kill. Flanked by two security guards who read the counter his rights, he asks the player to take his business elsewhere, advising him that from this point on, he will not be allowed to play blackjack in this casino. And so ends another battle in a war that started in Las Vegas twenty years ago.

9.

Gambling and Systems—Fantasies and Facts

HISTORY

Society's fascination with gambling is rooted in the attempts of prehistoric people to foretell their fate by divining the intentions of the gods. Dice were tossed for this purpose long before they were thrown to gamble, and thousands of years later, many still cannot mentally separate fate from games of chance. Just as the ancients believed that success or failure in life depended on the whims of the deities, the typical gambler today believes that his wins or losses are determined to a large extent by some supernatural force. I have studied gambling and gamblers for over twenty years, and I have found very few players who did not cling to at least one archaic superstition that had been mathematically disproven as long as three hundred years ago.

Since the decisions in games of chance were originally believed to be controlled by the gods, the study of the mathematics involved was at first considered sacrilegious. But by the sixteenth century, a number of scientists and mathematicians in response to queries by gamblers, usually noblemen, began analyzing gambling games. Gerolamo Cardano (1501–1576) wrote the first known book on mathematical expectations for games of chance; Galileo (1564–1642) was the first to publish an analysis of expectations for dice games, and Blaise Pascal (1623–1662) made a study of various gambling problems that led directly to the development of modern probability theory— an accurate indication of long-term expectation when results depend upon chance.

These probability theories are used by economists, physicists, biologists, and any number of scientists who find statistics indispensable to their research. In recent years, these techniques have been applied in the fields of insurance, economics, genetics, and engineering, to name just a few. But ironically the very people for whom these theories were developed—the gamblers—rarely acknowledge, much less accept them. Few gamblers have a grasp of the fundamental expectations for the game they play, and even these players often combine their knowledge with fallacies that frequently nullify it.

CHANCE VERSUS LUCK

The word "gambler" first appeared in print in eighteenth-century England, and the dictionary defines a gambler as one who wagers on an event. Chance is defined as the probability of an event happening, and luck has been defined as an apparent tendency to be fortunate or unfortunate. Here is where the problem starts. Most gamblers confuse "chance," which can be computed mathematically, with "luck," which is merely an apparent tendency—the key word being "apparent" as distinguished from "real." Chance plays an integral role in any gambler's expectation, but luck is an illusion.

FANTASIES

In 1977, Richard A. Epstein published his *Theory of Gambling and Statistical Logic,* which summarized all the theoretical and statistical work done on games of chance in the last 400 years and applied it to today's games. Additional, somewhat more specific information was also provided by Allan N. Wilson's *Casino Gambler's Guide,* published in 1965. Thus for more than fifteen years there has been no reason for gamblers to depend on guesswork or intuitive logic. But the following fantasies, identified in Epstein's book, are as widely held now as they were a hundred years ago.

• *A bet with a low probability of high gain is superior to one with a high probability of small gain.* Thus a 30-to-1 proposition bet on the craps table is better than an even-money wager on the Don't Pass Line, and in roulette a bet straight up on a number at 35 to 1 is preferable to wagering on red or black, regardless of the odds.

- *The probability of consecutive independent events is additive rather than multiplicative.* Hence the chance of throwing a seven on the craps table is twice as great with two throws as with one. If the chances for successive wins in a fair game are 1 out of 2, and 2 out of 4, then the chances are 3 out of 6, 4 out of 8, and 5 out of 10. In reality the chances are 3 out of 8, 4 out of 16, and 5 out of 32.

- *Everything will even out. After a streak of wins, the chances of losing increase.* If a craps 12 has not shown for a certain number of throws, it becomes a good bet. If in roulette red has not come up for a specific number of spins, black becomes a bad bet.

- *The probabilities of favorable events occurring are greater than unfavorable events of equal probability.* A person with one chance in a hundred of winning a pool and a 1% chance of dying from cancer feels that the former is much more likely to happen. Similarly, a gambler feels that his chances of winning a 20-to-1 bet are greater than his chances of losing his money in a proposition with a 5% risk-of-ruin factor.

- *The expectations for present events are based on past events, despite mathematical independence.* Thus in blackjack if you have broken every time you have hit sixteen that day, you should quit hitting sixteen regardless of what the dealer holds. If you have drawn poor cards in a number of double-down situations, stop doubling.

- *One large bet in a game is preferred to a series of small wagers totaling the same amount in the same game, but a series of small bets in different games is better than a single large wager in any of them.* Therefore a $100 bet in craps is better than four $25 wagers, but four $25 wagers, one each on blackjack, baccarat, roulette, and craps, are considered preferable to one $100 wager on any of them.

- *A group of additive bets is not very interesting, but a multiplicative bet is often worthwhile.* Three $5 bets on the favorites in three consecutive races are not considered very good, but a $15 three-horse parlay (if the first horse wins, all the payoff is bet on the second; if that horse wins, the total payoff is bet on the third) is considered an excellent bet.

- *Winning streaks extend long enough and happen frequently enough to counteract both losing streaks and intermittent losses.* If you progress your bets in a winning series, but make minimum bets in a losing series, you will win enough to offset both the losing series and the short-cycle losses.

- *A successful gambling session is the result of your superior skill, but a losing session is the result of bad luck.* When your spouse wins, however, it's because she was very lucky, and when she loses it's because she played badly.

- *Seeing is believing, so what you observe at a gambling game is a better basis for a playing strategy than what some mathematician writes in some book.* Maybe he has never even played the game. If betting all the hardways at craps and never splitting at blackjack have been winning for you, that must be the way to go.

- *Everybody has only so much luck, so be prepared to recognize it and use it to your advantage.* If you have been practicing with the dice at home and have thrown ten passes in a row, stay away from the casino; obviously you have used up your share of luck for the day.

- *There is no reason to be concerned about a proposition where you have only one chance in five hundred to get hurt.* As it's highly improbable that a blackjack dealer will not break once in nine hands, doubling up after each loss at a $2 table with a $500 maximum bet will surely make you a winner before the house limit wipes you out.

- *The power of positive thinking applies to gambling.* You can't make your point at craps or draw good cards in blackjack if you expect to lose.

- *Not only are some players inherently luckier than others, but this also extends to dealers and inanimate objects.* In blackjack, locate and avoid lucky dealers, and in craps search out hot tables and players with hot dice. Identify and refuse to bet on unlucky craps shooters.

FACTS

Just as the typical gambler entertains many, if not most, of the above fantasies, he also tends to ignore studiously the following facts, discussed to some extent in both Epstein's and Wilson's books.

- As the house has a definite edge in every casino game (except against card counters in blackjack), no betting system will break even in the long run, much less show a profit.

- For any casino game, every betting system will eventually reflect the inherent casino advantage for that game; therefore, no betting system is any better or any worse than all other betting systems, although systems with large betting ranges may lose faster.

- While it is true that the house has to continue to play indefinitely, and cover all bets within its stated minimum and maximum, the player derives no advantage from the option of varying his bets or quitting after a specific total win or loss, other than spreading his play over a longer period of time.

- Since every bet in every casino game has an edge for the house (except for the free-odds bets at craps), no combination of bets will show a profit for the player. It's impossible to combine a series of negative-expectation wagers and obtain a positive result.

- Because the casino advantage works on every bet, you have the best chance of doubling your money if you put your entire stake on the first wager, and then quit. The greater the number of bets you make, the more certain you are to lose your stake, and the less chance you have of doubling it.

LAW OF AVERAGES

Much of the gambler's childlike faith in his latest fool-proof betting system is brought about by a misunderstanding of the law of large numbers, misnamed the law of averages, and believed to mean that all things will eventually balance out, or "even up." For example, if you flip an unbiased coin long enough, an equal number of heads and tails is bound to appear. Nothing can be further from the truth. In his *Casino Gambler's Guide*, Allan Wilson defines the law of large numbers this way: "The greater the number of trials, *the smaller will be the percentage fluctuations* away from the expected, but *the larger will be the absolute fluctuations.*

In other words, if you flip a silver dollar 100 times, probability theory tells us that 95% of the time heads will appear between 45 and 55 times, 5 more or 5 less than the expected 50, or a 10% deviation. The same theory, however, says that in 10,000 trials 95% of the time heads will show between 4,950 and 5,050 times, 50 more or 50 less than the expected 5,000, but only a 1% deviation. Furthermore, if you flip a million times, heads will turn up 500 more or 500 less than the expected half-million, or just one-tenth of 1% off.

It is important to understand that the longer you flip the coin, the greater the number of times you will vary from an even split, but the closer you will be percentage-wise. Remember that just the percentage difference tends to even up, and then only after a tremendous number of trials, while at the same time the fluctuations in outcome get larger and larger.

BETTING SYSTEMS

Now that we have purged ourselves of our gambling fantasies, memorized the pertinent facts, and mastered the intricacies of the law of large numbers, we are ready to investigate betting systems. We now know two things a system cannot do:

- No system can guarantee a winning session.

- No system can, in the long run, overcome the casino advantage.

The question is: What can a betting system do? Three things:

- A system can make a gambling session more interesting and exciting.

- It can give you the most action for your casino dollar.

- It can enable you to capitalize on a winning streak and go home a winner!

Let's examine some of the more well-known betting systems.

WHICH SIDE TO BET

Every casino table game except blackjack offers some bets that can be expected to win about half the time. These near-even-money propositions include banker or player in baccarat; red or black, odd or even, and high or low in roulette; and pass or don't pass and come or don't come in craps. While some players, especially in craps, never vary their choice, other players, especially in baccarat, experiment with systems that would exploit a streak of wins for either choice. The simplest way to get on a streak is to bet on what won last, but if you were playing this way in baccarat, for instance, and banker then player won alternately, called chopping, you would soon be wiped out.

Avant Dernier

To overcome this problem, the *Avant Dernier* (French for before last) system was developed. This means you bet not on the last winning position, but on the one before that. This way you will capitalize on a win streak for either side as well as a streak of alternate wins. Of course, if a series of two consecutive banker wins then two player wins develops, known as double chopping, you will have problems.

Maturity of Chances

Although this system for deciding on what to bet is applied to some extent by baccarat enthusiasts and optimistic craps shooters, especially hardway bettors, *Maturity of Chances* systems are used primarily by roulette buffs. At a single-zero game, we know that in the long run an even-money bet will win 18 out of 37 times, a 2-to-1 bet will win 12 out of 37 times, a single number will win 1 out of 37 times, and so forth for all the ten roulette wagers. Now, if you care to extend long-run probabilities to the short run, try making small waiting bets on any even-money proposition, while keeping track of the results of every spin and watching for patterns to develop, such as a single number not appearing for 100 spins, a split number not appearing for 70 spins, or even red not appearing for 4 spins. Identifying the propositions that have occurred less frequently than expected, sometimes called sleepers, and then making larger than normal wagers on them, can be a fascinating way to play roulette. Casino personnel never object to this type of play, and, in fact, some casinos provide paper and pencils. An easier way to record the results of several hundred spins is to record them on a preprinted sheet, similar to the form on pages 172 and 173. Sample sheets, plus instructions for using them, can be obtained at no charge by sending a stamped self-addressed envelope to Gil's Guide.

HOW MUCH TO BET

The simplest answer is the same wager every time, betting an amount based on your bankroll that will enable you to play as long as you like. Known as flat betting, most of the time this method will result in small wins, small losses, or you will break even. If, however, you want the excitement of larger bets and a chance for a big win while controlling your losses, you'll need a "system," which can be defined as a plan that you will follow in response to any betting situation, ignoring hunches or emotions. Here are some of the most popular.

Martingale

Bet 1 unit after every win, but double the last bet after every loss until a win occurs, which will recover all your losses plus one unit.

The oldest, best-known, and possibly the worst system is the *Martingale,* used by Egyptian pharaohs as far back as 3500 B.C. and named after the proprietor of an early London casino who would constantly encourage his patrons to "double up and catch up." This betting method produces a series of small wins punctuated by occasional extremely high losses. Inevitably the system breaks down when a series of losses either runs you out of money or requires a bet higher than the table maximum.

Anti-Martingale

Bet 1 unit after every loss, but increase your bet after every win. As the name implies, you bet minimum after you lose, but double up after every win. Carried to its conclusion, you would keep doubling up until you finally lose, but because of this absurdity, nobody uses a pure *Anti-Martingale.* Instead you modify this betting method by limiting the number of doubled bets, by increasing the bet by something less than double, or by a combination of both. For instance with a series of wins you might bet 1 unit, 2 units, 4 units, 8 units, and then stay at that level until you lose. Another variation would be bets of 2 units, 3 units, 5 units, 7 units, and so forth until you lose or reach a maximum—either yours or the table's.

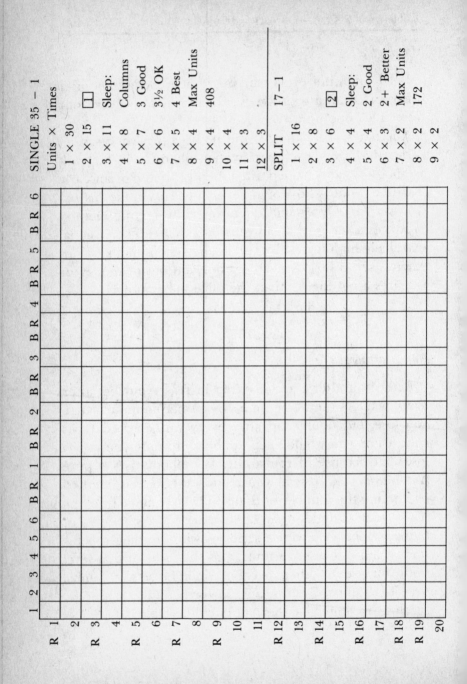

SINGLE 35 – 1

Units × Times

1 × 30	
2 × 15	1
3 × 11	Sleep:
4 × 8	Columns
5 × 7	3 Good
6 × 6	3½ OK
7 × 5	4 Best
8 × 4	Max Units
9 × 4	408
10 × 4	
11 × 3	
12 × 3	

SPLIT 17 – 1

1 × 16	
2 × 8	
3 × 6	2
4 × 4	Sleep:
5 × 4	2 Good
6 × 3	2+ Better
7 × 2	Max Units
8 × 2	172
9 × 2	

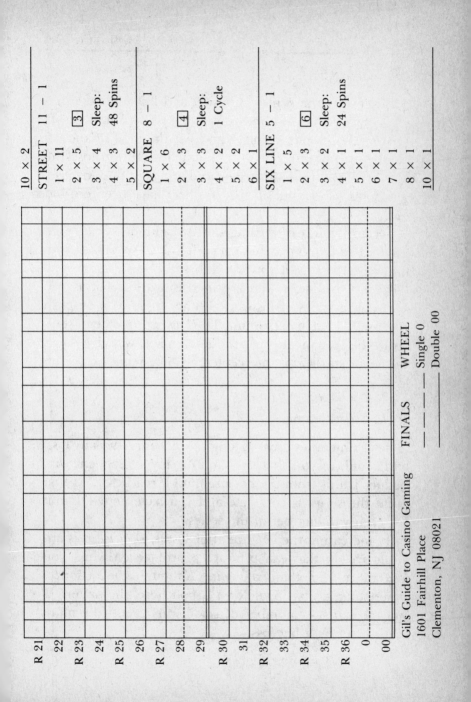

10 × 2

STREET 11 – 1

1 × 11
2 × 5   3
3 × 4   Sleep:
4 × 3   48 Spins
5 × 2

SQUARE 8 – 1

1 × 6
2 × 3   4
3 × 3   Sleep:
4 × 2   1 Cycle
5 × 2
6 × 1

SIX LINE 5 – 1

1 × 5
2 × 3   6
3 × 2   Sleep:
4 × 1   24 Spins
5 × 1
6 × 1
7 × 1
8 × 1
10 × 1

R 21
22
R 23
24
R 25
26
R 27
28
29
R 30
31
R 32
33
R 34
35
R 36
0
00

Gil's Guide to Casino Gaming   FINALS
1601 Fairhill Place
Clementon, NJ 08021

WHEEL
——— Single 0
— — — Double 00

Labouchere (Cancellation)

Always bet the sum of the first and last numbers in a series such as 1-2-3-4; in this case 1 + 4 = 5-unit bet. If you win, cross out 1 and 4 and bet the total of the remaining numbers; 2 + 3 = 5-unit bet. If you lose the first bet, 5, add the loss to the end and continue with the series 1-2-3-4-5 until all the numbers have been crossed out.

Because you are crossing out two numbers with each win and adding only one with each loss, in theory you can lose more bets than you win and still be successful. The fallacy, of course, is you are increasing your bet as you lose, and a series of losses can either break you or push you past the table maximum. The *Labouchere* system, similar to the Martingale but at a slower pace, will give you a cluster of small wins intercepted at some point by a large loss.

D'Alembert (Pyramid)

Bet 1 unit and repeat as long as you win. After any loss, add 1 unit to your bet size, and on any subsequent win, deduct 1 unit from the bet size until it reaches 1. At that point the series is complete and you have netted 1 unit for each winning bet in the series.

By increasing the bet size after losses, *D'Alembert* is another system that can produce a profit even when you lose more bets than you win. Although the action is slower than a Martingale or a Labouchere, the pattern is still the same—a number of small wins eventually more than offset by a big loss.

Paroli

Bet 1 unit and repeat as long as you lose. After any win, double your bet and add 1. Continue this until you either reach a predetermined level or lose, then start again.

More aggressive than the Anti-Martingale, where you bet all or part of a winning wager plus the original bet, *Parolis* usually produce big wins or none at all. The degree of boldness is up to the player, but a Paroli of Three is the most common. Here you bet 1-3-7, and if successful you draw down and start again, pocketing a profit of 11 units. Less aggressive players might bet 1-3-6, risking and winning 1 less unit.

MONEY MANAGEMENT

For players of casino games with an immutable house advantage, money management consists of a program that will give you the most play for your gambling dollar, while controlling your losses and offering some chance of winning and keeping a significant amount. Open to infinite variation, an acceptable program should include:

• Bet size—a minimum and maximum bet scaled to stretch your playing bankroll over the length of time you desire to play.

• Stop loss—a predetermined point beyond which you will not go, regardless of how fast you lost or how much time remains to play.

- Win goal—A predetermined amount, ideally related to your stop loss, that you will pocket and not risk in further play, again regardless of how fast you win or how much time remains to play.

If your gambling trip will cover several days, consider a stop loss and a win goal for each day, and resolve not to add pocketed winnings from one session to the bankroll for subsequent sessions. Play for pleasure and consider your losses a cost of entertainment.

A BEGINNER'S LIBRARY

Although hundreds of books have been printed about gambling, few of them are of any value to the novice gambler. If you are interested in good basic information about casino games, I recommend the following, listed in alphabetical order:

Casino Games by Bill Friedman (Golden Press; New York; 1973; $1.95)

The Casino Gambler's Guide, enlarged edition, by Allan N. Wilson (Harper & Row; New York; 1970; $12.95)

The Facts of Baccarat, revised edition, by Walter I. Nolan (Gambler's Book Club; Las Vegas; 1976; $1.50)

The Facts of Blackjack, revised edition, by Walter I. Nolan (Gambler's Book Club; Las Vegas; 1976; $1.50)

The Facts of Craps, revised edition, by Walter I. Nolan (Gambler's Book Club; Las Vegas; 1976; $1.50)

The Facts of Roulette, revised edition, by Walter I. Nolan (Gambler's Book Club; Las Vegas; 1978; $1.50)

Winning at Casino Gaming by the staff of Rouge et Noir (Rouge et Noir; New York; 1975; $11.95)

For a catalog of currently available books on gambling, write to: Gambler's Book Club, 630 South 11th Street, Box 4115, Las Vegas, Nevada 89106.

AN AGGRESSIVE CRAPS SYSTEM

I am a lifetime winner at craps. Although I don't play very often—counting cards at blackjack is much more profitable—I have won more money than I have lost ever since I first learned to roll the dice many years ago. This can be attributed to a combination of the vagaries of chance and an aggressive betting system which I'll share with you.

- Make a three-unit Pass Line bet with each new shooter.

- If a craps is rolled, replace the bet.

- If a natural is rolled, press* the bet.

- If a number is rolled, take maximum odds and make a three-unit come bet.

- If a craps is rolled before the Pass Line number is made, replace the come bet.

- If an eleven is rolled before the Pass Line number is made, press* the come bet.

*Press progression: 3-5-7-10-15-25-35-50-75-100-150-200

- After every new come number, take maximum odds and replace the come bet.

- After a Pass Line number is made, press* the bet, announcing, "Odds work on the come-out roll."

- If a natural is rolled after a Pass Line number is made, repeat the bet level once.

For even more aggressive play, press the come bets after each come number is made, but just repeat the pressed come bet after an eleven is thrown. I strongly suggest that you do not attempt this system in the casino until you've practiced many hours at home with a craps layout, dice, and chips. You'll have action on every roll of the dice and you'll need experience in keeping track of all the bets and progressing according to schedule. I risk 100 units in a regular game, and 150 units in a double-odds game. I quit when I've doubled my stake, but only after the shooter has finished.

*Press progression: 3-5-7-10-15-25-35-50-75-100-150-200

10.

Tournament Strategies

The tournament strategies described in this chapter were developed for the "Sands World Championship of Casino Games Tournament" held in Atlantic City in December 1981. They are, however, usable for other casino games tournaments held at any other hotels in Nevada and Atlantic City. The strategies are also usable by the gambler for his or her normal gambling sessions.

There are risks involved in any game of chance. The author cannot assume the responsibility for any losses incurred, nor does he expect any remuneration for success as a result of applying any strategies described in this book.

A WINNING OBJECTIVE

Most gamblers lose because they walk into a casino with no game plan and no objective of winning. They have a certain amount of cash in their pockets and are prepared to risk the entire amount in the hope of reaping a huge windfall. They overbet. And they end up losing.

If you wish to become a winner, you must establish discipline in your gambling sessions. You must set an objective for an amount you wish to win. You must define a limit or stop loss on the amount you are prepared to lose. These amounts must be consistent with your overall bankroll.

This chapter is written for gamblers. If you are a blackjack card counter who gambles, i.e., you play the other games and/or overbet your blackjack bankroll, you should study its contents carefully.

A gambler should understand that a winning session is based on three interrelated factors:

- A knowledge and use of percentages, i.e., those bets with the lowest house advantage;

- Careful and disciplined money management;

- Chance.

The careful combination of these factors into a game plan will provide the gambler with a higher probability of a winning session. But wins and losses run in cycles and are unpredictable. There is never a guarantee of winning. That's why a disciplined gambler will quit when he or she reaches a preestablished stop loss.

Caveat: The strategy described herein *does not* provide you with the means of overcoming the house advantage. No strategy will do that except card counting at blackjack. It will provide you with a good chance of going home a winner, but not every time. As long as chance is involved in our equation, there is no way to predict what your exact chances are of coming out ahead. You will do all right if you study this chapter carefully and adopt the philosophy of "why not quit winners?"

HOW TO APPROACH THE CASINO GAMES TOURNAMENT

Your game plan for a Sands-type multiple Casino Games Tournament should include a decision to risk the $2,000 buy-in amount, not on one tournament game but over all four games. You will risk $500 (or 25% of your bankroll) on each of the four tournament games: blackjack, craps, roulette, baccarat. If you lose the $500, you will withdraw from the tournament, replenish your $2,000 buy-in bankroll with the lost $500, and wait for the next tournament to begin.

Therefore, if you plan on entering all four tournaments, which I recommend, you must have $3,500 cash available. But the most you can lose is $2,000.

If you are advancing in the Blackjack Tournament, have won one or more rounds, you may cash in your blackjack buy-in amount to enter one or more of the other tournaments. You will be given a receipt at the end of your round for the total money you have accumulated. Take this to the cashier's cage and they will cash it in for you. Then you have your $2,000 cash to buy-in for the next tournament (e.g., craps). You will, of course, be expected to buy in for $2,000 cash when you enter the next round of the Blackjack Tournament.

If you intend to seek a group of friends to chip in and help you finance the $2,000 buy-in, then you should agree to share both your table winnings and prize winnings proportionately to how much they invest. For example, if you invest $1,000 and each of your two friends invests $500, then you would keep half of your total winnings and they would each receive 25%.

OVERALL TOURNAMENT STRATEGY AND TACTICS

Risk no more than $500 per tournament entered.

Do not stack your chips in neat piles, especially if you are close to or in the lead! Keep them messy. This will make it difficult for the other players to determine how much to bet as they attempt to catch you. On the other hand, you should always know how much money you have in front of you—especially near the end of each round.

Try to hold back on your bets until all the other players have made theirs. This will allow you to bet more if you are attempting to catch someone, and give the other players as little information as possible as they attempt to catch you. You can fool the other players by picking up a stack of greens, for example, when you intend to bet only two, and then dropping the two bottom ones from the stack onto the betting layout.

Get a good night's sleep before you play. Avoid alcohol and eat a well-balanced meal on the day of play. You want to be totally alert.

Study and follow the playing and betting strategies in this chapter. Make up small cards to help you remember. Keep these cards in your pocket and study them between rounds. Do not hesitate to use them during a round if it will aid your play. Just make sure you don't hold up the game.

BLACKJACK TOURNAMENT STRATEGY

In the Blackjack Tournament, 60 hands are played per round. Your playing and betting strategies will be associated with the beginning game (first 20 hands), middle game (second 20 hands), and end game (third 20 hands). There is also a strategy for the last few hands if you are close to or in the lead.

Your playing and betting strategies will deviate from normal because you must be prepared to take risks for a short run of 60 hands. Each deviation from basic strategy is mathematically sound—you have the advantage over the dealer or a near 50-50 play on that hand. Your basic strategy advantage is greater than the indicated deviation, but remember, we are playing for the short run, and our objective is to get as much money on the table as possible by doubling and splitting at the appropriate times.

Your playing and betting strategies are also dependent upon whether or not your stake is above or below $2,000 and whether or not you are hopelessly behind or have a good shot at winning your round. If your bankroll dips below $2,000, your goal is to preserve your bankroll and get out of the round even or losing no more than $500.

When you are money ahead (playing with the house's money, as gamblers call it, but not really, because you have won it and it now is on your side of the table), you can afford to take some risks.

Beginning Game (First 20 Hands)

- Play basic strategy—no deviations.

- High-low (2–6 = +1; 7–9 = 0; 10–A = −1) counters bet $2 per running count for first two decks played, $3 per running count for second two decks played, and $4 per running count when dealer deals from last two decks. Do not bet more than $50 per hand.

- High-Count players (see the end of this chapter for a description of the High-Count System) use a $5 betting unit. Do not bet more than $50 per hand.

- Other players use a progressive betting system keyed to a short count. In a seven-player game, you will see, on the average, 22 cards per round. If you count fewer than eight high cards (tens, pictures, aces) in each round, press your bet $5 on each successive win. If you count eight or more, bet the same amount as on the last hand—do not press. Do not bet more than $50.

- If you lose $500, withdraw from the tournament.

Middle Game (Second 20 Hands)

- Make no changes if your buy-in amount is below $2,000; if you lose $500, withdraw from the tour- nament.

- When you are ahead, add the following *double down* plays to your playing strategy:

Your Hand	Dealer Up-Card
8	5 or 6
9	2 or 7
11	A
A,2 or A,3	4
A,8	3,4,5,6

Add the following *pair splits* to your playing strategy:

9,9	7
10,10	2,3,4,5,6,7

- Take insurance on a blackjack.

- High-Low counters bet $5 per count when the count is +5 or higher. Or bet progressively in a series of wins as follows (but only if the count remains above +5): $25, 25, 50, 50, 75, 75, 100, 100 (max). Revert to $25 or $5 times count on a loss. If the count is 0–5, bet $3 per count or progressively on a series of wins: 5, 5, 10, 10, 15, 20, 25 (max). Revert to $5 on a loss.

- High-Count players adopt a similar betting strategy to above depending on whether the actual count is below normal ($25 progression), around normal ($10 progression), or above normal ($5 progression).

- Short-Count players (counting only the high cards in each round) use a similar betting strategy to that of

High-Low above: $25 progression if high cards are fewer than 8; $10 progression if high cards are 8 or 9; and $5 progression if you count more than 9 high cards in the round just dealt.

End Game (Last 20 Hands)

- If your bankroll is less than $2,000, make no changes. Play the strategy described in the Beginning Game.

- If you lose $500, withdraw from the tournament.

- When you are ahead, add the following double-down and splitting plays to your playing strategy (in addition to those in the Middle Game) *only if you are attempting to catch up*. If you are on or near the lead, do not add these plays.

Your Hand	Dealer Up-Card	Decision
9	8	Double
10	10,A	Double
A,2; A,3; A,4; A,5	3	Double
A,6; A,7	2	Double
A,8	2,7,8	Double
A,9	4,5,6	Double
10,10	8,9,10,A	Split

- Insure all blackjacks. If you are in or near the lead, insure your hands totaling 20.

- If you are on or near the lead, do not change your betting strategy from the Middle Game.

- If you are behind with a chance at catching the leader, change the progressions in the Middle Game from $25 (+5 or more), $10 (0–5), $5 (negative count) to $50 (+5 or higher), $25 (0–5) and $10 (minus count).

- If you start losing while using this aggressive betting strategy and your bankroll dips below $2,000, you must decide realistically whether you still have a shot at catching the leader. If you do, continue betting in the same way but remember to honor your $500 stop loss. The only time you would play beyond the stop loss is if everyone else is losing too and you're close or in the lead with an excellent chance of winning.

End Game (Last 6 Hands)

Your playing and betting strategy for the last six hands will be determined solely by whether or not you are in the lead or close to the leader.

- If you have a comfortable lead—$500 or more—play conservatively and do not double or split on *any* hand. You don't want to risk losing your lead. Bet according to the Beginning Game strategy.

- If you are in the lead, you must watch your opponents like a hawk. Especially watch your opponents who are playing to your right—they play their hands first. If a player who has a chance to catch you breaks his hand, stand on all stiff hands no matter what the dealer's up-card is. On the other hand, if this player is pat or draws to a standing hand on a dealer 7–A, you must do the same and risk breaking.

• If you are close to the lead, you must bet and play these last six hands as aggressively as possible in an attempt to catch up. Try to size your bet according to the leader's bet. You must split any pair or double down on any two-card total if you have a reasonable chance at winning the round.

CRAPS TOURNAMENT STRATEGY

As noted above, a winning strategy, whether it be for tournament play or a normal gambling session, is based on three factors: percentage play, money management, and chance.

For the Craps Tournament, our overall strategy will be to make only percentage bets with the lowest casino advantage until the End Game (with one exception, to be discussed below), and then only if we are ahead with a good shot at winning.

We will confine ourselves to pass-line, don't-pass, come, and don't-come bets for the beginning (first 40 completed rolls) and middle (second 40 completed rolls) games. We will always take full odds and let our odds bets work on the come-out roll. In the end game (last 40 completed rolls) we will use place betting if we are playing catch up with a shot at winning.

Craps is a game of cycles, and we will try to use this factor to get us riding on the right cycle—do- or don't-side betting—at the right time.

Remember, a $500 loss means a withdrawal from the tournament.

Now, let's get down to the details.

Beginning Game (First 40 Completed Rolls)

Your first bet is $5 on don't pass. Now notice the other players' bets. Most players will probably bet the pass line with follow-up come or place bets. Your strategy is to go against the crowd, bet the don't side and hope for "cold dice" in the beginning of your round. Then, when most pass-line bettors are getting discouraged, you will shift over to the pass line and hope the table turns hot.

Here is your don't-side betting sequence:

- Bet $5 on don't pass. Lay full odds, i.e., lay $6 to win $5 if point is 6 or 8; lay $10 to win $5 if point is 4 or 10; lay $9 to win $6 if point is 5 or 9.

- Make two and only two don't-come bets and lay full odds as above. If the shooter sevens out, remember to pick up your winning don't-come bets when the dealer pushes them to the don't-come bar.

- Do not press your bet on a loss, i.e., if the shooter makes his point. Keep betting the same amount. Do not press your bet on a come-out win, i.e., a 2 or 3.

- If two shooters in succession seven out, i.e., you win, then press your bet, i.e., bet $10—on both don't pass and don't come. Continue to lay full odds. Remember we are hoping for a cold table. I have seen the dice quickly flow all the way around the tables with shooter after shooter sevening out. Continue to press your bet by $5 each successive win. Your progression looks like this: $5, 5, 10, 15, 20, 25, 30, 35, etc.

- If you lose one or both don't-come bets during a shooter's roll, don't make another don't-come bet until after your new point has been established. Continue to bet the don't side as long as you are winning, i.e., the dice are don't-passing. If a shooter makes two passes in a row, together with numbers, i.e., you are losing both don't pass and don't come, shift over to the pass line. But if your don't-come bets are still intact, bet against the shooter for a third time. If the shooter makes three passes in succession, this is your signal to lay off this shooter and consider shifting to the pass line. If your don't-come bets are still working, lay off the shooter and make neither a pass nor a don't-pass bet.

If your don't-come bets have been lost, shift over and bet with the shooter—progression to be discussed below.

Continue to lay off the shooter as long as your don't-come bets are working. If he sevens out and you win both don't comes, stay with the don't side.

To summarize, you will continue to bet the don't side until a shooter makes three or more passes in succession and you have lost your last two don't-come bets.

When you shift to the pass line, you are committed to it for the remainder of the round.

Your pass-line betting sequence is the same as the don't side; i.e., press on successive wins after the second: $5, 5, 10, 15, 20, 25, etc. Your come pressing works the same way. Always take full odds on the pass-line and come bets. Remember when you are betting three units, i.e., $15, you can back it with $20 for points of 5 and 9 and $25 for the 6 and 8.

Always let your odds work on the come-out roll.

Middle Game (Second 40 Completed Rolls)

If you are still betting on the don't side, do not change your game until you shift over to the pass line, as described in Beginning Game above.

If your bankroll has dipped below $2,000, do not change your game. Continue betting as in Beginning Game above.

Remember to withdraw if you lose $500.

If you're betting the pass line and your bankroll is above $2,000, your betting strategy changes for the Middle Game.

You will continue with your pass-line and two-come-bet strategy. But you are going to bet that the shooter *can make two passes in succession.**

You start by betting $10 on the pass line and making two $10 come bets—all with full odds of course.

Now suppose the shooter passes and suppose you have two come bets out, each with $10 odds. You have a total of $40 riding on the come.

You bet an amount equal to your total come plus odds bets—in this case, $40—on the pass line. You let your odds bets work on the come-out roll. You protect your $40 pass-line bet with a $5 or $6 Any Craps bet.

Now let's see what can happen. The best thing would be for the shooter to throw one of your come numbers. You win. If the shooter throws a seven, you lose both come bets but you recoup the full amount on the pass line for a break-even situation. If the shooter throws Any

---

*I learned this strategy from Joe V.—a professional blackjack player who likes to gamble at craps.

Craps, you lose your pass-line bet but recoup it with your Any Craps bet. If the shooter throws an eleven, fantastic. Just remember to replace your Any Craps bet. Any other number thrown is your new point and you continue with your sequence.

Your come-bet progression on successive wins is as follows: $10, 15, 20, 25, 35, 50, 75, 100, etc.

Your pass-line progression follows your come-bet progression.

While you are waiting for the shooter to make his point, add up the total dollar value of your two come bets with odds. *This is your next pass-line bet.*

After the shooter makes his point you must do the following in rapid succession:

- Divide your next pass-line bet by seven to get the value of your next Any Craps bet, e.g., $40 ÷ 7 = $5 or $6. Toss this bet to the stickman in the center while the dealer is making his payoffs.

- Pick up your winning chips and make your new pass-line bet.

- Announce to the dealer: "Let my odds work." You must do this before each come-out roll.

If the shooter throws a seven on the come-out roll— wiping out your come bets—you have one of two choices:
  (1) Revert to a $10 or $15 pass-line bet and start progression over;
  (2) Go with the shooter's streak and continue to bet the same amount on the pass line.

Choose option (1) if you are in or near the lead. Option (2) should be exercised if you are attempting to catch up.

End Game (Last 40 Completed Rolls)

With 14 players around your craps table it will be difficult to estimate the amount of money the other players have won. Many of the other players may be trying to confuse you, just as you are trying to confuse them.

But pay attention all through the round. Watch the size of their bets. Notice who is pressing up and winning—if anyone. Try to determine who has the most black chips. This is the player you want to catch.

If you are in the lead or near the lead, you don't want to change your game. The Middle Game strategy can win you a lot of money quickly.

As usual, you will make no changes if your bankroll is less than $2,000. We want you to conserve your bankroll and take a shot at roulette.

The only reason for changing your strategy in the End Game is if you must attempt to catch the leader and you are in a position to use money you have won to do so.

If you are more than $500 behind and you are attempting to catch up, shift to place betting.

Your pass-line progression will start at $15 and progress as follows: $15, 20, 25, 40, 50, 75, 100, 150, 200, 300, 400, 500, 750, 1,000, etc. You will continue to take full odds.

For each new shooter you will place the 6 and 8 for $30 each. The money from your first two wins will be used to place the 5 and 9. Following that, you will press the 6 and

8 to $60 and the 5 and 9 to $50. Now take the profit from each number for one bet, i.e., 6 and 8 return $70; 5 and 9 return $70.

At this point, go "all the way up" on each of these four numbers, i.e., when the 5 or 9 hits, toss the dealer a $5 chip and say, "All the way up." You now have your original $50 plus your $70 win plus $5, for a total of $125 riding on each of these two numbers. Your payoff, should either hit again, is $175.

For the 6 and 8, press to $120. Press $60 of your $70 win and take down the other $10. A $120 place bet on the 6 or 8 pays $140.

So far we have been playing an inside (i.e., 5,6,8,9) number strategy. If the shooter's point is one of these numbers, you ignore it, i.e., bet the other three numbers, as described above.

Here is the way your progression looks:

5 and 9: $25, $50, $50, $125
6 and 8: $30, $30, $60, $120

When you take down the money from a $100+ bet, the first thing you do is "buy" the 4 and 10 for $25 each.

These bets will cost you $1 each for "juice" but pay off at 2 to 1. You then progress the 4 and 10 as follows (on successive bets, of course):

$25, $50, $75, $100, $150, etc.

Your inside numbers progress as follows at bets above $100 after the first win:

5 and 9: $250, $250, $500, $500, $1,000
6 and 8: $240, $240, $480, $600, $990

The above, of course, is predicated on a hot shooter and there is a very small chance that you will ever see these kinds of pro-

gressions. But you must be prepared in case they do occur. And you will be taking down profits on every other hit. You must bet aggressively if you are attempting to catch the leader, and the above approach is about as aggressive as you can get within the confines of disciplined money management.

When the shooter sevens out, revert to your original bets to start the progressions, i.e., $15 on the pass line and $30 each on the 6 and 8.

Be sure to protect your pass-line bets by betting one-seventh the amount on Any Craps.

If this strategy brings you close to the leader—as best you can judge—don't be afraid to take down your place bets. If taking down your place bets will bring you about even with the leader or close enough to have a shot for the final six rolls, take them down and start your progression over, i.e., $15 pass line and $30 each on the 6 and 8.

End Game (Last 6 Completed Rolls)

If you are in the lead, become conservative. Stay with your place-bet strategy but don't progress as aggressively. Take down all your place bets before the final roll.

If you are fighting for the lead, take no profits, i.e., press your bets up to the limit as quickly as possible—if this is possible during the last six rolls. For example, if you are sitting as follows prior to the last six rolls:

4 and 10: $25 each
5 and 9: $125 each
6 and 8: $120 each

Progress as follows:

    4 and 10: 25, 75, 225, 600, 1,000
    5 and 9: 125, 250, 500, 1,000
    6 and 8: 120, 240, 480, 990

You are playing catch up and you are playing for the last roll.

ROULETTE AND BACCARAT TOURNAMENT STRATEGIES

Gamblers have been attempting, for hundreds of years, to devise infallible betting systems for roulette, betting systems in which your next bet is predicated on a prior sequence of wins or losses. All of these systems, except one, have failed and have bankrupted hundreds and probably thousands of gamblers who dreamed of striking it rich in the casinos. They have failed because of a common fallacy—increasing one's bet to cover all or a portion of prior losses.

For example, the oldest of these systems—the Martingale—requires the gamblers to double their bets on each successive loss until a win and then return to a one-unit bet. The gambler risks his entire bankroll to win one unit! Consider the following losing sequence: 1, 2, 4, 8, 16, 32, 64, 128, 256, 512. If the gambler possesses the necessary 1,023 units to cover this losing sequence, he bumps against the house maximum of 500 units in attempting to make the tenth bet. Most gamblers go broke long before they reach the house maximum. And ten losses in a row just isn't that uncommon.

If you have been using such a system and winning, you are "dancing between the raindrops." It is just a matter of time before you blow your entire bankroll.

But there is a way to turn the use of a progressing betting system to your advantage. In my twenty-five years of gambling research, this particular strategy is the only progressive betting method I have found that frequently works. No, it won't overcome the house advantage. But still you can use it to win with the necessary patience and discipline.

It combines the three elements we require for our Tournament Strategy: percentages, money management, and chance. It does add a fourth—patience—so I debated for quite some time before incorporating it into this Tournament Strategy.

But, in all due diligence, I firmly believe that this system* provides you with the best shot at winning not only the Roulette and/or Baccarat Tournaments, but in coming home a winner from your normal gambling sessions as well.

The method is elegant in its simplicity. It is based on Labouchere betting progression which looks like this: 1, 2, 3, 4.

In a normal Labouchere progression, the gambler bets the sum of the two outside numbers. He crosses these two numbers off on a win or adds the amount of his bet to the series on a loss. A sequence of wins and losses—

*Documented in Norman Leigh's *Thirteen Against the Bank*.

W,L,L,L,L,W,W,L,W,W—would present the following
line: *1, 2, 3, 4, 5, 7, 9, 11, 12*.

We have won five times and lost five, crossed out the
series, and won 10 units (the sum of all numbers in the
original series).

The gambler is duped into thinking that he has an infallible system because he can win fewer times than losing
or win about half the time but still make money. But we
know it doesn't work that way and so did Norman Leigh
as he masterminded the scheme described so eloquently
in *Thirteen Against the Bank*.

The essence of the scheme: We reverse the progression
and force the casino to play the system as we play the
casino. We increase our bets and add numbers to the series as we win instead of as we lose. Losses are used to
cross the number off. Thus our same sequence of wins
and losses as above (W,L,L,L,L,W,W,L,W,W) would produce now the following line: *1, 2, 3, 4, 5*.

The third loss in the above sequence wipes out our series because we cross off the two outside numbers for
each loss and add the amount of our bet on a win. So we
start a new series thus: *1*, 2, 3, 4, 5, *7*, 8, 11.

The above line would result from the end of the above
sequence: L,W,W,L,W,W. Our line stays alive, keeps ex-
tending itself on a series of dominant wins. We are playing with money won and our bets keep getting larger.
Let's continue the above series with the following sequence: W,W,L,W,W,L,L,W,W,W—*1, 2, 3, 4, 5, 6, 7, 8*,
11, 14, *17, 19, 24*, 25, 36, 47.

Our objective is to keep the line open by picking one
even-money bet (roulette: red, black, odd, even, 1–18,

19–36; baccarat: players or bank) and sticking with it.

If losses force you to cross out a line, you have lost 10 units $(1+2+3+4)$ and you start over with a fresh line.

Your objective on any line is to reach the table maximum bet—in this case, $1,000. If you are lucky enough to reach the table maximum, you are finished with your line and return to a new 1, 2, 3, 4, and a 5 unit—in our case $5—bet.

Now, I admit that you are going to cross out many series and incur many 10-unit losses before you will experience one that will take you to table maximum. But that one series often will more than compensate for all your prior losses.

And you have just as good a chance at getting your series during the tournament round of 70 spins (roulette) or 80 hands (baccarat) as any other time.

Here is how to play the reverse Labouchere (or "Reverse Labby," as Leigh affectionately called it in *Thirteen Against the Bank*) in the tournament:

For the beginning game (first 25 spins at roulette; first 30 hands at baccarat), assign the value of $1 to your units. Your series 1, 2, 3, 4 consists of 10 $1 units and you are never betting less than the $5 minimum $(1+4$ or $3+2)$.

You must pick an even-money bet: red, black, odd, even, high, low at roulette or players or bank at baccarat. This is purely a subjective decision on your part except for baccarat. I recommend going with the players. That way you avoid the 5% commission on your wins on the bank side (which would increase your 10-unit loss for each series).

In roulette when the house green comes up you lose

half your bet. Leave the other half out on the same bet and don't count it as a loss unless you lose that half on the next spin. Don't count it as a win unless you win the next two times.

If you have a series going as you approach the Middle Game, do not change units until your series is either crossed off or extends itself to the table maximum.

When you start a fresh series in the Middle Game, increase your unit to $5, i.e., multiply the sum of your two outside numbers by $5 to get your bet size. Your first bet in the starting series of 1, 2, 3, 4 will now be $25 instead of $5, and you are now losing $50 per crossed-off series instead of $10. This aggressive approach should be used only for tournament play and not for your normal gambling sessions.

Remember that your stop loss is $500 and to withdraw from the tournament if you hit that number.

In the End Game (last 20 spins at roulette, last 20 hands at baccarat), you must decide whether or not to back off from a winning line before you get to the table maximum. I recommend that you consider backing off only during the last six plays, and then only if you have a substantial lead and don't wish to risk losing it. Even then, backing off may be dangerous unless your lead is insurmountable.

HOW TO USE THE STRATEGIES FOR NORMAL GAMBLING SESSIONS

Every strategy in this chapter is usable in your normal gambling sessions!

You divide your session into a beginning, a middle, and an end game. Your division will be based on money won instead of completed hands, rolls, or spins. I will develop this concept later in this section.

You then decide how much you wish to risk for your gambling trip, e.g., $1,000. Divide that by the number of days in your trip. For example, if you are going down for the weekend, you should allocate $333 for your Friday-evening sessions, $333 for your Saturday sessions, and $333 for your Sunday sessions.

If you plan to gamble three hours on Friday evening, then you could play a "day bankroll" of $333.

Now, pick your game and play the strategies as described herein. If you are losing, you make no changes— you play conservatively. If you are winning, you can play more aggressively and shift over to middle- or end-game strategies as developed below.

If you lose your day's bankroll, you quit for the day. If you lose your trip bankroll, you quit for the trip. Do not cash checks and do not use credit. Lose only the money that you have decided to risk.

Key Decision 1: Your Winning Objective

You must make one key decision about your gambling trip—what is your winning objective? How much do you wish to win? I recommend that you select one of the following five options:

(1) Win 20% of your bankroll, then quit;
(2) Win 50% of your bankroll, then quit;
(3) Win 100% of your bankroll, then quit;
(4) Keep playing if you reach your selected objective (1–3) above but establish a 20% backoff or stop-loss amount;
(5) Use in conjunction with key decision—see below.

Let's take a $500 trip bankroll as an example:
• For option (1), you quit if you win $100.

• For option (2), you quit if you win $250.

• For option (3), you quit if you win $500.

• For option (4), set $20 as your stop loss for Option (1)—you risk 20% of your $100 win; $50 as a stop loss for Option (2) or $100 as a stop loss for Option (3).

Key Decision 2: How Aggressively Do You Wish to Play

The second key decision you must make is how aggressively you wish to play, i.e., should you shift over to a middle-game or end-game strategy.

You may make a decision not to shift over at all, especially if you are close to or have met your winning objective.

If you plan to shift over to a middle- or end-game strategy, you will be playing much more aggressively and you need a bigger win before you make the shift. Let us now establish option (5) for your winning objective:

(5) Win 100% of your bankroll, then shift to a middle-game strategy. Risk your entire win and shoot for another 100% win. For the $500 bankroll example, you would shift over on a $500 win. You plan to win another $500. You quit if you lose the $500 you won, i.e., you quit even.

We can now define option (6) for a winning objective:

(6) If you've hit your second 100% win, i.e., you've re-doubled your bankroll, shift to an end-game strategy and risk only the second 100% that you've won. If you lose that, quit and go home with your doubled bankroll.

Remember, you don't have to shift over to either a middle- or end-game strategy. You will be playing very aggressively and risking everything that you've won. There is a good chance that you may lose all of your winnings!

On the other hand, if you're going to take a shot at a big win, this is the time to do it—when you're playing with money won.

Special Comment to Blackjack Players

If you are hesitant about playing the Tournament Playing Strategy for the middle and end games, just shift over to the more aggressive betting strategies. I am not recommending that you deviate from basic strategy for your normal gambling sessions. But this is a book for gamblers and not blackjack purists. If you're going to gamble by taking a shot with my strategy variations, you are still playing against less of a casino advantage than playing craps, roulette, or baccarat.

ADAPTING THE STRATEGIES FOR ANY CASINO GAMES TOURNAMENT

Although the strategies herein were developed for the Sands World Championship of Casino Games Tournament in Atlantic City, they are adaptable to any tournament in any casino.

If you are entering a tournament with only a single game, e.g., Sahara Blackjack Tournament, you would risk the entire buy-in amount instead of 25% of it as described herein.

If you are entering the Sahara Blackjack Tournament, use the playing and betting strategies exactly as described herein, except divide your two-hour round into a beginning (first 40 minutes), a middle (second 40 minutes), and an end (last 40 minutes) game.

If you are entering a Craps Tournament, e.g., the Riviera or Resorts, use the playing and betting strategies exactly as described herein. Just define your beginning, middle, and end games according to tournament criteria (time or completed rolls).

Roulette and Baccarat Tournament players follow the same principles.

THE HIGH-COUNT SYSTEM

You have the advantage when the remaining deck(s) is rich in 10's and aces. That's when you should increase your bet.

The High-Count System was developed for the player who does not wish to invest the time required to learn the more complicated strategies. Counting high cards only is much easier than scanning every card to update a point count.

You play this system by counting 10's and aces and watching the discards or discard tray. You must be able to approximate the remaining deck(s) in the game. This is done by estimating the discards and subtracting this number from the total deck(s) in the game, e.g., in a six-deck game if you estimate one deck is in the discard tray, then there are five decks remaining.

Select and learn the appropriate table for the game you will be playing. Bet one unit when the total count of the high cards seen is normal or above. When fewer than normal high cards have been seen, bet according to the table.

This system approximates betting one unit per High-Low true count, and will be slightly off whenever a surplus of 7's, 8's, and 9's has been played.

Exhibit 12:
High-Count-System Tables

Six-Deck Game

Remaining Decks	Normal Count	Actual 2-Unit Bet	Count 4-Unit Bet	6-Unit Bet
5	20	10	0	
4	40	32	24	16
3	60	54	48	42
2	80	76	72	68

Four-Deck Game

Remaining Decks	Normal Count	Actual 2-Unit Bet	Count 4-Unit Bet	6-Unit Bet
3	20	14	8	2
2	40	36	32	28
1	60	58	56	54

Eight-Deck Game

Remaining Decks	Normal Count	Actual 2-Unit Bet	Count 4-Unit Bet	6-Unit Bet
7	20	6		
6	40	28	16	4
5	60	50	40	30
4	80	72	64	56

A SIMPLIFIED BETTING METHOD

Your high bet should not exceed 2% of your casino bankroll; that is the total of the money you have set aside to play blackjack. Divide the high bet by the number of units at the high bet to determine your unit bet and table minimum. For example, if your bankroll is $1,500, in a six-deck game your high bet would be $30 (2% of $1,500), and your unit bet would be $5 ($30 divided by 6). You should play at a $5-minimum table.

Caution: This system is not as effective as the High-Low Point Count System. Your long-run advantage with High Count is about 0.5% as compared to about 1.5% for the Point Count Systems.

Exhibit 13:
Gamblers' Money-Management Tables

Roulette and Baccarat (Use this table in conjunction with the Reverse Labouchere Strategy described in this chapter.)

Betting Bankroll	Betting Unit	No. of Losing Series	Loss per 1 2 3 4 Series
$ 500	$ 1	50	$ 10
$ 2,500	$ 5	50	$ 50
$ 5,000	$10	50	$100
$12,500	$25	50	$250

Gamblers' Money-Management Tables

Craps (Use this table in conjunction with the betting strategies described in this chapter.)

Bankroll	Betting Unit	Odds Bets			Come Bets	Session Bankroll	Progression
		4,10	5,9	6,8			
$ 500	$ 3	$ 3	$ 4	$ 5	2 per	$ 100	1 unit per
$ 750	$ 5	$ 5	$ 6	$ 5	shooter	$ 150	successive
$ 1,500	$10	$10	$10	$ 10		$ 300	win after
$ 2,500	$15	$15	$20	$ 25		$ 500	2nd win
$ 3,750	$25	$25	$30	$ 25		$ 750	
$ 7,500	$50	$50	$50	$ 50		$1,500	
$11,250	$75	$75	$80	$125		$2,250	

11.

Casino Gaming Services Offered by Jerry L. Patterson

This section is promotional in nature. Because I am committed to and believe in what I am doing, I have included in this chapter a description of all the gaming services I offer. I invite reader inquiries on all the services described below.

THE INSTANT ADVANTAGE®

During the last several years, while teaching over 4,000 gamblers how to win at blackjack, it has always been my goal to strip the mystique from card-counting techniques; to simplify these techniques so that occasional players can enjoy an advantage over the casino and win money seven times out of ten. My students (and my track record) attest to my success: 90% are consistent winners. (I know this because I poll my students as part of a comprehensive follow-up program.)

My teaching techniques make learning easy and fun.
Simple drills and exercises are used. No memory or math
ability is required. About twenty to thirty hours of practice are required to become a skilled card counter.

Practice, however, is the key word. Many occasional
gamblers just don't want to invest either the time or
money (my twelve hour course, described below, costs
$450) to develop these skills, or the time required to keep
them sharp once they are acquired. So, I've developed
the revolutionary Patterson Short-Count Method, which
can be learned in minutes and used immediately to
achieve the Instant Advantage® over the casino.

- There is nothing to remember from hand to hand.

- There is forward counting only—no minus counts or
  up and down counting.

- Your counting range per hand will vary from one to
  ten.

- There are only two simple calculations. Each relates to a
  natural number that is self-evident at the blackjack table.
  The elegant simplicity of the Short-Count Method relates to these two natural numbers. Anyone can walk up
  to a blackjack table and notice them at once.

- You compare one natural number to a count of the
  high cards on this hand to determine whether or not
  you have the advantage on the next hand.

- If you have the advantage, you use the other natural
  number to determine your bet size.

It's that simple. That's why I call it Instant Advantage®, because you actually gain an instant advantage over the casino. All you need do is read the five page description, go to the casino, and start winning right away. (If you don't know the basic strategy, you'll need to practice about an hour to learn my eleven simple rules of how to play the hands.)

The Patterson Short-Count Method works with any number of decks: one, two, four, six, eight, or more. In a multi-deck game, you wait a little longer before you raise your bet, but I show you how to do that by using one of the two natural numbers.

Casinos enjoy up to a 20% advantage over the average, losing gambler. That's $20 out of every $100 you bet. That's like throwing your money away. With my method you first eliminate the casino advantage and save that $20 per $100 bet, then you gain up to a 1% advantage and gain $1 per $100 bet. Even with a small bankroll, your bets can add up to a lot of $100 bets per hour. And small bankrolls add up to larger bankrolls if you let your winnings ride by plowing them back into your bankroll.

I'll even teach you some simple tricks the pros use to maximize their winnings, such as how to read the dealer's hole-card (in Nevada and Caribbean casinos); when to sit down and when to leave a table; when to take insurance; even a simple technique to adjust your count and bet to reflect the decks remaining to be played.

I would not put my name on this system if it didn't work. My Blackjack Clinic, discussed below, has been permanently located in the Philadelphia/southern New Jersey area since 1978, and is recognized as the best blackjack school in the country. And, while the Blackjack Clinic is the only way to get the best advantage possible over the casino, the Instant Advantage® system provides the simplest, fastest way of insuring that your next trip to the casino won't be a losing one.

THE BLACKJACK CLINIC

The Blackjack Clinic is a blackjack school which I own and operate. Twelve hours of instruction are delivered to the student over a four-week period—three hours, one night a week, for four weeks. This same class is offered on a weekend basis with a four-week follow-up service in cities throughout the country. There are a number of unique and extraordinary features about the Blackjack Clinic. Here are just a few:

- The students actually win money (I know this because I poll them every three months).

- Anyone can learn to win because I have stripped the mystique from winning blackjack methods (our students come from all walks of life: insurance agents, truck drivers, construction workers, housewives, self-employed businessmen, retired persons, etc.).

- The program is continuous—follow-up service includes a joint visit to a casino, an open line to me and my instructors, periodic review sessions and blackjack updates, and a blackjack newsletter.

Why, you may be asking, should I take your course on blackjack instead of just reading your book on blackjack? There are a number of reasons you should consider it.

- It is difficult to learn from any book, my own included. In a book you can learn what winning blackjack is all about, but the key is *how*. How to play basic strategy perfectly without even thinking about it. How to count cards swiftly and accurately. How to bet to maximize your profits and minimize your chances of going broke. How to avoid getting barred.

- The keys to learning how to win are the drills and exercises. In the Blackjack Clinic, there are seven basic strategy drills, nine card-counting drills, and two money-management drills. Doing these drills is easy and fun. You record your progress and gain a keen sense of accomplishment as you watch your skills develop.

- It has been proven that a person learns faster and more effectively in a classroom environment. There are a limited number of students per class, and each receives all the individual attention he or she needs from me or one of my personally trained instructors. If you need a makeup session, you get it. If you need extra help, you come in early or stay late. If you have a question during the week, you call your instructor or my office. An 800 line is available.

- Beginning to intermediate players will especially benefit from the Blackjack Clinic, although quite a few advanced students have taken it to "fine-tune" their game. No one is held back and each progresses at his own rate of speed.

- Practice is extremely important. We program your home practice sessions while you take the Clinic.

If you want further information, just check the appropriate box on the request form at the end of the book. An outline of the course is contained in the Appendix.

THE ADVANCED BLACKJACK CLINIC

Learning how to count cards and using this information to vary your bet size are all you need to know to win at blackjack. You learn this in the Blackjack Clinic. Serious students of the game, who are playing semiprofessionally or professionally and desire to "put the icing on the cake," enroll in the Advanced Clinic and learn to gain a small but significant (in terms of dollars won) additional advantage. The following are the highlights of the Advanced Clinic I offer to my graduates and to other qualified students:

- You learn that the running count becomes more significant as the shoe is dealt out and the number of decks remaining to be played decreases.

- You learn to use this information to compute a true count used for variations to the basic strategy and more precise betting decisions.

- You learn to obtain a small but powerful additional advantage by counting aces and using this side count for making more precise insurance, strategy, and betting decisions.

- You learn about the power of team play and why the casinos fear well-trained blackjack teams.

If you wish further information, check the appropriate box on the request form at the end of this section. An outline of the course is contained in the Appendix.

BLACKJACK CORRESPONDENCE COURSE

My first book—*Blackjack: A Winner's Handbook*—sold 12,000 copies in its first two printings. The readers of this book are beginning and intermediate blackjack players from all parts of the country and from foreign countries as well. Many of them have just as much interest in learning to play blackjack the right way as students in this area. Many of the readers wrote to me asking for additional information about my Self-Instruction Course.

Because of this interest I was motivated to duplicate the Blackjack Clinic for use outside my own geographic area. But it had to be done right. I had to personally get involved with each student. Because of its interactive nature, a correspondence course with telephone consultation was the only vehicle that would accomplish this objective.

Thus the Blackjack Correspondence Course was born. It has proved tremendously successful and has assisted hundreds of students to become winning blackjack players. Here are the highlights:

- You can work at your own rate of speed in the privacy of your own home.

- Winning blackjack cannot be learned by reading books. You will gain invaluable practical experience before risking your money in the casinos.

- The entire body of blackjack data is presented to you in an orderly fashion to simplify the learning process.

- You are not working alone. You have access to me at all times via telephone or written correspondence.

- The skills that you will achieve are measurable and as you record your drill performance, you will see these skills increasing, e.g., you will learn to count down a single deck in less than thirty seconds.

- Once you have achieved your desired level of skills, you decide upon the winnings you want to achieve. My unique money-management methods will show you how to achieve your desired level of winnings.

- The one most-heard comment from my students is that they are impressed with my honesty, integrity, and genuine desire to develop them into accomplished, moneymaking Blackjack players. This is why I schedule a joint visit to the casino to observe and comment on your play where it really counts—under actual casino conditions.

The Blackjack Correspondence Course is divided into four levels and nine lessons as follows:

Level 1: Skilled Blackjack Player
  1. The Basic Strategy—How to play the hands.
  2. The High-Low Point Count System—How to count.
  3. Basic Money Management—How to bet.
  4. Casino Comportment—How not to get barred.
Level 2: Intermediate Blackjack Player
  5. Intermediate Blackjack Techniques—How to maximize your winning advantage.
Level 3: Advanced Blackjack Player
  6. Variations on the Basic Strategy—How to use the true count to play the hands.
  7. Advanced Money Management—How to bet with the true count.
  8. Side Count of Aces—How to use a side count of aces for playing and betting.
Level 4: Team Blackjack Player
  9. Team Play—How to multiply your winnings through team play.

Each lesson consists of:

• A detailed lesson plan including background information, complete instructions, assignment descriptions, and a statement of the skills to be achieved.

• Reading assignment.

• Memory aids.

• Drills—Written drill sheets as well as single- and multiple-deck drills.

- Essay assignment.
- Quiz.
- Questions and answers.

After you complete each lesson, you will send all materials to me for my written critique, which will be forwarded to you by return mail. Any out-points will be corrected and you will be able to achieve the projected skill level before you undertake the next lesson. You may stop after achieving your desired level of play—you pay for only those lessons you decide to take.

For further information, check the appropriate box on the request form.

BLACKJACK CLINIC FRANCHISES

Because of the success of the Blackjack Clinic, I am expanding into other areas. The franchise holders I am seeking must be successful blackjack players and have some business and teaching experience.

What better source than my own students? I have struck a profitable balance between teaching and playing that I am confident I can duplicate in other individuals in other areas just as I have with students in this area.

Two former students operate a franchise in Ohio. Another, who also holds a full-time job, manages New York City and Long Island. The states of California, Texas, Michigan and Wisconsin are being developed as this is written, and operating Blackjack Clinics are available. It's pretty much up to you what you want to do.

Now, here is what I can do for you.

1. I will teach you to become a Skilled, Intermediate, Advanced, and then a Team Blackjack Player through the Blackjack Clinic, Advanced Clinic, or the Blackjack Correspondence Course.
2. I will present you with a Blackjack Clinic franchise plan. This plan will show you how, *in your spare time*, you can build a successful Blackjack Clinic in your own area. You and I will be partners, and I will be right there during the key start-up period to help you implement all of my organizational and instructional materials. Much of the marketing for your area will be done centrally—through my books and magazine and newspaper columns.

CASINO GAMES CLINIC

There are, of course, other casino games besides blackjack. The major difference is that there is no permanent way to overcome the long-term casino advantage in craps, roulette, baccarat, the slot machines, or the Big Six Wheel.

Recognizing that there are many players who have an interest in these other games—mainly craps, roulette, and baccarat, where the house advantages are the smallest—I offer a Casino Games Clinic. You may enroll for classes in craps, roulette, baccarat, or in any combination of the three. Each of these three classes also features a lesson in blackjack's Basic Strategy. The highlights of this clinic are detailed in the Appendix.

If you are interested in the Casino Games Clinic, check the appropriate box on the request form.

COMPUTER-ASSISTED
BLACKJACK TUTOR

Custom-designed for use with the relatively inexpensive TRS-80 Model 3 Computer, the Computer-Assisted Blackjack Tutor will enable a player with just elementary knowledge of basic strategy, card counting, and money management to become a highly skilled blackjack player. The program includes the High-Low counting system, easiest to learn, easiest to play, used by more players than any other system and rivaling the most advanced count for efficiency. The player may set parameters to describe the type blackjack game he wishes to play: number of decks, number of players, cut-card placement, money-management strategy, and many others.

Working at your own pace, in the privacy of your own home or office, you can gain invaluable experience and achieve any desired level of expertise before risking your money at the tables. The Computer-Assisted Blackjack Tutor features three types of drill and practice aids. Each is discussed below.

Basic Strategy Drill: The player can set indicators to allow him to play any kind of hands:

- The player can ask for random cards to be dealt against random dealer's up-cards.

- The player can fix the dealer's up-card and play random hands.

- The player can ask for pairs or double-down hands to be dealt against fixed ranges of dealer up-cards.

- The player can play soft hands only against fixed or variable dealer up-cards.

The computer remembers those hands giving the player problems and increases the frequency of the problem hands. Any errors are immediately corrected. The player is given a second chance to get the right answer before the computer communicates it to the player.

The player can also play a blackjack game drill and specify the number of hands to be dealt per round and the number of hands to be played by the player. The computer plays the others. A full recap is given at the end of the session.

Card Counting Drill and Practice: The card counter can have the cards shown to him at variable rates of speed. The object is to keep the count as fast as the cards flash on the screen.

The player can play a one- to seven-player game drill and play any or all of the hands; the computer plays the others. The player can specify the speed at which the cards are dealt and whether or not the computer will check for basic strategy errors. The player can request to see the correct count at the completion of each hand.

Money-Management Drill and Practice: The player can bet one hand. The computer checks for a correct bet size according to a prescribed money-management formula which considers the count and the amount to be bet per count together with the player's maximum bet and bankroll.

See and use this program with a fully qualified instructor at the Blackjack Academy at One Britton Place, Voorhees, New Jersey, before you buy. For further information, just check the appropriate box on the request form.

CASINO GAMBLER'S NEWSLETTER

If you would like to stay abreast of where to find favorable rules, i.e. double odds at craps, single zero at roulette, and double down after splitting at blackjack, you will be interested in subscribing to this newsletter. The cost will be repaid many times over just by keeping you up-to-date on junket information (free trips to casinos all over the world for a day, a weekend, or a full vacation). This newsletter will keep you abreast of the many casino games tournaments that are sponsored by casinos in both Atlantic City and Nevada. Rules of play, prize structures, and playing strategies will be covered in depth.

Bibliography

Arnold, Peter. *The Encyclopedia of Gambling*. London: Quarto, 1977.

Baldwin, Roger, Wilbert Cantey, Herbert Maisel, and James McDermott. *Playing Blackjack to Win*. New York: Barrows & Co., 1957.

Barstow, Frank. *Beat the Casino*. Santa Monica: Carlyle Assoc., 1979.

Braun, Julian H. *How to Play Winning Blackjack*. Chicago: Data House Publishing Co., 1980.

Epstein, Richard A. *The Theory of Gambling and Statistical Logic*. New York: Academic Press, 1977.

Friedman, Bill. *Casino Games*. New York: Golden Press, 1973.

Goodman, Mike, and Michael J. Goodman. *Your Best Bet*. New York: Ballantine Books, 1977.

Humble, Lance, and Carl Cooper. *The World's Greatest Blackjack Book*. Garden City, NY: Doubleday & Co., 1980.

Leigh, Norman. *Thirteen Against the Bank*. New York: Morrow, 1976.

Noir, Jacques. *Casino Holiday*. Berkeley, CA: Oxford Street Press, 1970.

Nolan, Walter I. *The Facts of Baccarat*. Las Vegas: Gambler's Book Club, rev. ed., 1976.

————. *The Facts of Blackjack*. Las Vegas: Gambler's Book Club, rev. ed., 1976.

————. *The Facts of Craps*. Las Vegas: Gambler's Book Club, rev. ed., 1976.

————. *The Facts of Roulette*. Las Vegas: Gambler's Book Club, rev. ed., 1978.

O'Neil-Dunne, Patrick. *Roulette for the Millions*. Chicago: Henry Regnery Co., 1971.

Patterson, Jerry. *Blackjack: A Winner's Handbook*. Voorhees, NJ: Casino Gaming Specialists, 1977. Revised and expanded edition, New York: Perigee Books, 1982.

————. *Blackjack's Winning Formula*. Voorhees, NJ: Casino Gaming Specialists, 1980. Revised and expanded edition, New York: Perigee Books, 1982.

Renzoni, Tommy. *Renzoni on Baccarat*. Secaucus, NJ: Lyle Stuart, Inc., 1973.

Rouge et Noir, staff. *Winning at Casino Gaming*. Glen Head, NY: Rouge et Noir, 1975.

Scarne, John. *Scarne's Guide to Casino Gambling*. New York: Simon & Schuster, 1978.

Scharff, Robert. *The Las Vegas Expert's Guide*. New York: Grosset & Dunlap, Inc., 1968.

Squire, Norman. *How to Win at Roulette*. London: Pelham Books, Ltd., 1968.

Thorp, Edward O. *Beat the Dealer*. New York: Random

House, 1962. Revised version, New York: Vintage Books, 1966.

Uston, Ken. *Million Dollar Blackjack.* Los Angeles: SRS Enterprises, 1981.

Wiley, Dean. *Money Management in the Casino.* Las Vegas: Gambler's Book Club, 1978.

Wilson, Allan N. *The Casino Gambler's Guide.* Enlarged edition, New York: Harper & Row, 1970.

Winkless, N. B. Jr. *Gambling Times on . . . Craps.* Hollywood: Gambling Times, Inc., 1981.

Wong, Stanford. *Professional Blackjack.* Las Vegas: Gambler's Book Club, 1977. Revised version, New York: William Morrow and Co., 1981.

Appendix A.

Jerry Patterson's Blackjack Clinic Outline

Lesson 1: Basic Strategy
Introduction
Overview of the Clinic
- Blackjack's Winning Formula
- Importance of Practice
- Clinic Procedures
- Recommended Books

The Basic Strategy
- Background
- Explanation of Blackjack Decisions, How the Game Is Played, Hand Signals
- Discussion of the Basic Strategy
- Discussion of Multicard-Hand Decisions

Drills
- Basic-Strategy Flash Cards
- Basic-Strategy Matrix Drill

- Ten Commandments
- Playing Record
- Betting Tables

Casino Comportment
- Handling Your Emotions
- How to Avoid Getting Barred

Drills
- Multicard-Hand Drill
- Minus-Count Drills
- Betting Drills

Play Blackjack with Chips

Lesson 4: Professional Blackjack Techniques
Questions and Answers
Money-Management Review Questions
Intermediate-Zone Betting
Plowback Strategy
Factors and Techniques Which Affect Your Winnings
- Intermediate Variations to the Basic Strategy
- When to Take Insurance
- The Importance of Bet Spread and Cut-Card Placement
- Back-Counting and Walking on Negative Shoes
- Playing More Than One Hand
- Team-Play Techniques
- Tips to Identify Dealer's Hole Card

Drills
- Six-Deck, Seven-Hand Blackjack Game Drill
- Model Practice Session

Play Blackjack with Chips

Appendix B.

Jerry Patterson's Advanced Blackjack Clinic Outline

Lesson 1: Variations to the Basic Strategy with the True Count

Introduction

Overview of the Clinic
- Importance of Practice
- Clinic Procedures
- Recommended Books

Variations to the Basic Strategy
- Why, When, and How to Vary the Basic Strategy
- When to Take Insurance
- How to Compute a True Count by Estimating Remaining Decks
- Gradient Approach to Learning the Variations

Drills
- Deck-Estimation Drill
- Computing the True-Count Drills

- True-Count Decision Drill
- Rounding Drill
- Deck-Variation Drill
- Variation Flash Cards
- Six-Deck Countdown Drill
- Variations-Matrix Drill

Play Blackjack

Lesson 2: Optimal Betting and Money-Management
   Strategy
Questions and Answers
Matrix-Drill Review
Strategy-Variations Review Questions
Optimal Betting with the True Count
- How to Bet with the True Count
- How to Size Your Bets According to Your Bankroll
- Discussion of True-Count Betting Table
- How to Achieve a 20-to-1 Betting Spread
- How, When, and Why to Use "Stop Losses" and "Win
   Stops"

Drills
- Rounding Drill with Betting
- Blackjack Game Drill with Betting
- Table-Variation Drill

Play Blackjack

Lesson 3: How to Play Blackjack Around the World
Questions and Answers
Matrix-Drill Review
Money-Management Review Questions
World Blackjack
- "The Blackjack Formula"

Appendix C.

Jerry Patterson's Casino Games Clinic Outline

Craps
- How to Play—the rules and the procedures
- How to Bet—the best bets and the worst bets
- How to Win—and how to take it home
- How to Keep From Going Broke—ride out that losing streak
- How to Select a Craps System—to fit you and your bankroll

Roulette
- How to Play—the rules and the procedures
- How to Bet—the best bets and the worst bets
- How to Select a Game—single zero and surrender
- How to Select a System—for playing and betting
- How to Use Team Play—minimize risk and maximize profit

Baccarat
- How to Play—the rules and the procedures
- How to Bet—banker or player
- How to Select a System—for playing and betting

Blackjack
- How to Play—the rules and the procedures
- How to Eliminate the House Advantage—up to 6%
- How to Play Basic Strategy—split, double, hit, and stand correctly
- How to Select a Betting System—go home a winner

Appendix D.
Jerry Patterson's Blackjack Clinic Locations

Jerry L. Patterson's Blackjack Clinic is offered in the following regions:

• Mid-Atlantic Region

Classes are offered in the greater Philadelphia area; New Jersey; Pennsylvania; Delaware; Baltimore; Washington, and in Virginia and the Carolinas.

Address: The Blackjack Clinic
         One Britton Place
         Voorhees, NJ 08043
Phone: New Jersey (609) 772-2721
       Toll Free   (800) 257-7130
Contact: Nancy Patterson or Walter Jaye

• Northeast Region

Classes are offered in the greater New York City area, including Manhattan; Long Island; Westchester and Rockland counties and all of New England.

Address: The Blackjack Clinic
            10 Arbor Lane
            Bardonia, NY 10954
Phone: (212) 410-3508
            (914) 623-0661
Contact: Don Schlesinger or Kenny Feldman

• Southwest Region

Classes are offered in the greater Los Angeles area; central and southern California; Phoenix; and New Mexico.

Address: The Blackjack Clinic
            One Britton Place
            Voorhees, NJ 08043
Contact: Nancy Patterson or Walter Jaye

• Midwest Region

Classes are offered in the Youngstown, Cleveland, Akron –Canton, Columbus and Cincinnati, Ohio, areas.

Address: P.O. Box 1306
            Warren, OH 44482
Phone: (216) 394-5221
Contact: Mike Stauffer or Doug Devine

Classes are offered in the Chicago, Illinois; Madison and
Milwaukee, Wisconsin; and Minneapolis–St. Paul, Min-
nesota, areas.

Address: 5718 Norfolk Drive
                Madison, WI 53719
Phone: (608) 271-4921
Contact: David Gerisch

Note: The Northwest, Central, and Southeast regions are
being organized as this book goes to press. Franchises
are available in all regions.

Appendix E.

Casino Gaming Equipment and Supplies

For the casino gamer interested in setting up his own practice and play facilities at home or at the club, there is an excellent source of gaming supplies and equipment available in the Philadelphia/south Jersey area—Gil's Guide to Casino Gaming.

Gil offers handsome, sturdy, and fold-up blackjack tables for low discount prices. You may even order the table with the Atlantic City basic strategy imprinted on the layout. There is also available an authentic-looking craps table.

Gil also offers dealer's shoes, casino-like chips, discard holders, blackjack and craps layouts, and many other fine products—all at discount prices. Write directly to Gil for a free catalog: Gilbert E. Stead, Gil's Guide to Casino Gaming, Dept. QP, 1601 Fairhill Place, Clementon, NJ 08021. Telephone: (609) 228-7277.

About the Authors

Jerry L. Patterson, syndicated gaming columnist, is the author of *Blackjack's Winning Formula* and *Blackjack: A Winner's Handbook.* His casino-gaming column, appearing weekly in the *Philadelphia Bulletin* and the *Trentonian,* has been published in the New York *Daily News,* the San Francisco *Chronicle,* the Philadelphia *Inquirer,* the Baltimore *Sun,* the *South Jersey Courier Post,* and the Atlantic City *Press.* In addition, his articles have been printed in the *Boardwalker, Chips,* and *Millions* magazines.

Mr. Patterson, nationally known teacher of winning blackjack methods, is the founder and operator of the Blackjack Clinic, a school that has instructed nearly 4,000 students in Blackjack's Winning Formula in its first four years of operation. An active professional blackjack player, playing and winning in casinos all over the world, Jerry has spoken out in behalf of the occasional gambler on dozens of radio and TV talk shows, as well as on a number of TV news programs.

* * *

Walter Jaye, professional blackjack instructor and expert player, has taught hundreds of people all over the United States how to play a winning game, both in person at the Blackjack Clinics and through the Blackjack Correspondence Course, which he directs. He has taught the basic course, the advanced course, and the team course, and has managed several successful blackjack teams for Jerry.

Walter was also responsible for much of the research, analysis, and rewriting of the newly revised and expanded edition of Jerry's very popular *Blackjack: A Winner's Handbook*.

Copy this form and send to:

Jerry Patterson
P.O. Box 3040
Carson City, NV 89702

Information Request Form
For faster service call Toll Free: 1-800-257-7130

Dear Jerry,

Please send me information on the following:

[ ] Blackjack/TARGET 21 Method. Send me a 12-page brochure on this Home Study Course with audio and video tapes.

[ ] Blackjack Classes in casino cities which use the casinos as a learning laboratory.

[ ] The Jerry Patterson Network and Network Newsletter for Casino Gamblers

[ ] Send a wallet-sized blackjack Basic Strategy Card for:
       [ ] Atlantic City
       [ ] Las Vegas
       [ ] Reno and Northern Nevada

[ ] A professional level, winning craps method including a home study course and classroom instruction

[ ] A professional level, winning roulette method including a home study course and classroom instruction

[ ] Jerry, send me your Special Report on how you overcome the house advantage and win consistently in craps and roulette.

[ ] Information on your Sports Betting Investment Program for Football, Basketball, Hockey and Baseball; please include information for opening an account at a legal, off-shore sports book

[ ] Thoroughbred Wagering Service for Major Tracks

Name: _____

Street Address: _____

City/State/Zip: _____

Telephone Number with area code first: _____